PLAN B
HOW LEAVING THE EURO
CAN SAVE IRELAND

The Author

Cormac Lucey teaches finance at the Irish Management Institute, University College Dublin and Chartered Accountants Ireland. He is a chartered accountant. He has worked in various financial roles in banking and in industry in Ireland and in Germany and is a frequent media commentator on Ireland's economy. He served as special advisor to Michael McDowell during the 2002–07 government. He lives in Dublin with his wife and son.

PLAN B
HOW LEAVING THE EURO CAN SAVE IRELAND

CORMAC LUCEY

Gill & Macmillan

To Ciara

Gill & Macmillan
Hume Avenue, Park West, Dublin 12
www.gillmacmillanbooks.ie

© Cormac Lucey 2014
978 07171 6176 8

Typography design by Make Communication
Print origination by Síofra Murphy
Printed and bound by CPI Group (UK) Ltd, CR0 4YY

This book is typeset in Minion and Helvetica Neue LT.

The paper used in this book comes from the wood pulp of
managed forests. For every tree felled, at least one tree is
planted, thereby renewing natural resources.

A CIP catalogue record for this book is available from the
British Library.

5 4 3 2 1

CONTENTS

INTRODUCTION

Rarely do we find men who willingly engage in hard, solid thinking. There is an almost universal quest for easy answers and half-baked solutions. Nothing pains some people more than having to think.

Martin Luther King

It may seem odd, with the ECB, EU and IMF Troika having departed Ireland in December 2013, to call for a default on our debts and for exit from the eurozone. Instinctively, people don't want to do either of these things. For the first would involve reneging on debts freely entered into. The second would involve reneging on the European Union's current big project. And things are getting better, right?

Before we answer that question we need to decide if we want to start this discussion with an emotionally reassuring conclusion, seeking out facts which support that conclusion, or if we are genuinely open to varying conclusions depending on where the evidence leads us.

We must also remember the fundamental distinction between liquidity and solvency. Back in September 2008 our banks admitted that they suffered from a liquidity problem (they were unable to access cash), but they denied any solvency crisis (as the value of their assets exceeded the value of their liabilities). We now know that the main reason the banks were suffering from a liquidity problem in late 2008 was that they were fundamentally insolvent.

Currently the Irish economy is enjoying liquidity growth while fundamental questions about its underlying solvency remain unanswered. Thanks to a significant loosening of monetary policy

under European Central Bank (ECB) chief Mario Draghi, the amount
of money flowing around the economy is no longer declining. But
thousands of Irish households and businesses, and even the State
itself, remain threatened by the spectre of insolvency.

Although little noticed at the time, the replacement of Jean-
Claude Trichet by Mario Draghi at the helm of the ECB in 2011
proved to be very significant. By providing over €1 trillion of
cheap credit to Europe's fragile banks (through the Long-Term
Refinancing Operation mechanism), he ensured funding for banks
that might otherwise have been threatened by liquidity crises. The
economic effects of this measure – perceived as largely technical by
the general public – have been profound.

Pressure on distressed banks across the eurozone periphery,
i.e. Ireland, Portugal, Spain, Greece and Italy, has eased. And those
banks have used some of the extra funding they got to buy bonds
issued by their own governments. This has driven up the price of
government bonds across the periphery, pulling down their yields
and thus the perceived risk of national bankruptcy.

According to the November 2013 report of the German
Central Bank, or Bundesbank, Irish commercial banks increased
their holdings of Irish government bonds by 60 per cent between
November 2011 and September 2013. It was a similar story for other
countries on the eurozone periphery.

The Germans are highlighting this phenomenon because they
disapprove of it. They see it as back-door central bank financing
of government borrowing, something explicitly prohibited by
European treaty law. It also directly contradicts the June 2012
decision of euro area ministers, which sought 'to break the vicious
circle between banks and sovereigns'. Heavy bank purchases of
government debt actually reinforce the circle of interdependency
between banks and sovereigns.

But who in the corridors of power cares about such quibbles?
The reduction of financial crisis risk that comes from Draghi's
interventions has helped stem the outflow of deposits from Irish
banks. It has thus backstopped the liquidity of the Irish banking
system and the national economy. Allied to this, Irish residential
property prices have stopped falling.

So now, in December 2013, property prices are rising, employment figures are growing and the Troika is leaving. The leader of the Labour Party has even called for tax cuts for 'hard-pressed working families'. Is an end to our economic travails now in sight?

Hold your horses. Ireland still suffers from insufficient economic growth. As long as the interest rate on our debts exceeds our economic growth rate, our debts will grow faster than our underlying capacity to service them. And, for all the talk about 'green shoots', economic growth since 2007 has been persistently disappointing.

In a report on the Irish economy in 2013, the International Monetary Fund (IMF) warned that if the growth of real gross domestic product (GDP), i.e. our annual economic output adjusted for inflation, stagnated in the medium term, Ireland's debt would be unsustainable. The Department of Finance expects real GDP growth in 2013 to have been just 0.2 per cent. And, in November 2013, Ireland's official budgetary watchdog, the Irish Fiscal Advisory Council, warned that the probability of breaching the 2015 deficit ceiling of 3 per cent of GDP 'has risen from an estimated 1-in-3 to an estimated 1-in-2'.[1] Even in early 2014, there were several stark warnings that the eurozone crisis was not over:

- The President of the European Central Bank Mario Draghi dismissed as 'premature' upbeat comments from José Manuel Barroso, President of the European Commission, who had earlier predicted that the eurozone would put the crisis behind it in 2014.[2]

- Professor of Economic History at Oxford University Kevin O'Rourke wrote that 'An adjustment strategy based on the expectation that already over-indebted countries will pay back what they owe in an environment of falling prices seems doomed to failure; all the more so if "internal devaluation" at the level of individual member-states is replaced by euro-zone-wide deflation.'[3]

- The former head of the Bundesbank Axel Weber told the World Economic Forum in Davos that the underlying disorder continues to fester and that the eurozone is likely to face a fresh market attack this year: 'Europe is under threat. I am still really concerned. Markets have improved but the economic situation for most countries has not improved.'[4]

- The winner of the 2010 Nobel Prize for economics Sir Christopher Pissarides, who backed the euro when it was created but has since called for a break-up, said he thought the current more optimistic sentiment was premature. 'I don't think we're safe yet,' he said. 'European leaders such as [German Finance Minister Wolfgang] Schäuble are saying we're [getting] over the crisis [and] the euro is safe. I'm not confident yet.'[5]

- Leading economist Barry Eichengreen warned that it was 'much too early' to celebrate the eurozone's recovery. He also specifically warned that the reduction in interest rates on Irish government debt was more than that justified by the country's economic rehabilitation. And, for good measure, he stated that the entire crisis could blow up again in 2014.[6]

These gloomy assessments come even before we consider the appropriateness of comparing our debt to a GDP figure massively inflated by enormous US multinational profits, over which Ireland has no real claim. And they come before we consider gargantuan public pension liabilities that dwarf the official national debt figure.

Under such circumstances, the longing of Irish and EU authorities to declare victory may say more about the extent of their desperation than about our prospects for escape from the Economic and Monetary Union (EMU)-induced debt trap that we, and the rest of the eurozone periphery, are entangled in.

Today Ireland is rather like a heroin addict who got used to plentiful supplies of a dangerous drug – credit – at a very cheap price over the years running up to 2007. Since 2008, that drug has been withdrawn and our economy has been suffering economic cold turkey. The resulting human suffering has been enormous. Now, thanks to Mr Draghi, we have stumbled onto a supply of monetary methadone and things don't feel quite so bad. But the underlying debt and cost-competitiveness problems developed during the long period of our addiction remain largely untreated.

The symptoms may have been somewhat alleviated, but the disease remains substantially unhealed.

This book explains why Plan A, the authorities' plan to fix the economic problems of the eurozone periphery, cannot work and why we must instead apply Plan B, i.e. debt restructuring and eurozone exit. The book is organised into the following chapters:

1. **Is the Worst Behind Us?** – explains why, contrary to the expectations of many, the worst of this economic crisis may not be behind us, and therefore we may have to think the previously unthinkable in our search for an enduring solution to our economic problems.

2. **Boom** – explains in detail how Ireland's membership of the euro lies at the root of the economic bubble which Ireland experienced between 1997 and 2007.

3. **Bust** – outlines how the forces of the bubble went into an abrupt reverse to push Ireland into an economic bust.

4. **Plan A** – explains the measures taken by the authorities to combat the economic bust and why, as they are based on a fundamental misapprehension of the sources of the crisis, they are doomed to failure.

5. **Plan B** – sets out the two key measures required for Ireland's return to some sort of economic normality: debt restructuring and eurozone exit.

6. **Epilogue** – outlines the political backdrop to Plan B, accepting that Ireland is unlikely to implement the plan on its own and that therefore Ireland must be ready to join other eurozone members in finally exiting the doomed common currency area.

01 IS THE WORST BEHIND US?

The truth that makes men free is for the most part the truth which men prefer not to hear.

Herbert Agar

ARE WE NEARLY THERE YET? IS THE WORST BEHIND US?
Ireland's economy peaked in 2007. The following year, 2008, saw growing realisation that the country faced more than a blip or even a soft landing. In July of that year, Minister for Finance Brian Lenihan introduced spending cuts of €1 billion and argued that 'The sensible measures that I am announcing here today will create the right fiscal conditions for economic growth while protecting the most vulnerable.'[1] In September 2008, the government guaranteed Ireland's banks. This was done, according to the government, 'to maintain financial stability for the benefit of depositors and businesses and is in the best interests of the Irish economy.'[2]

A little over a year later, in December 2009, Brian Lenihan declared in his budget speech that 'the Government's strategy over the last eighteen months is working and we can now see the first signs of recovery here at home and in our main international markets.' He went on to conclude:

Yes, we have endured a traumatic eighteen months. The speed and ferocity of the recession has knocked us off our stride. But the innate advantages that brought us the boom have survived the downturn. We have taken a step back but we have in place a plan to take us forward on the path of sustainable economic growth....

Our plan is working. We have turned the corner. I commend this budget to the House.[3]

But when Irish voters went to the polls in February 2011, they clearly didn't believe that Ireland had 'turned the corner'. Lenihan's Fianna Fáil party suffered a catastrophic wipe-out as several cabinet ministers lost their seats; the party's Green Party allies managed to lose all of their seats. Brian Lenihan was the only Fianna Fáil candidate to win a seat in Dublin. That small electoral success may have been due to the fact that he was bravely fighting a battle with cancer, which was to cost him his life just four months later.

In the new Fine Gael–Labour coalition government, Lenihan was replaced as Minister for Finance by Michael Noonan of Fine Gael, and a new department, the Department of Public Expenditure and Reform, was carved out of the Department of Finance. Noonan, therefore, was to share his ministry with Labour's Brendan Howlin, the new Minister for Public Expenditure and Reform. Howlin and the Labour Party had campaigned aggressively against the outgoing government's economic policies and its subservience to the Frankfurt-based ECB, arguing that the choice facing the electorate was – as Labour leader Eamon Gilmore put it – between 'Labour's way or Frankfurt's way'. Noonan and the Fine Gael party had been more circumspect in their criticisms of the Fianna Fáil-led government, although Fine Gael's Spokesperson on Enterprise Leo Varadkar did say that 'not another red cent' would be put into Anglo-Irish Bank.

While in opposition, Fine Gael and Labour campaigned aggressively against their predecessors' economic policies and cooperation with the Troika. But, in government, they followed substantially the same policies.

By the start of 2014, the Fine Gael–Labour government was nearly three years in office and the people of Ireland had experienced five gruelling years of budgetary austerity. But there was little sign of a return to substantial economic growth. Ireland's banks remained in intensive care as total lending continued to contract. Ireland's national debt continued to spiral ever upwards. And only partial progress had been made in reducing the annual gap between government spending and revenue.

But this was not the message being delivered by Ireland's political masters. In a speech given to Financial Services Ireland on 4 July 2013, Michael Noonan asserted, 'We have a difficult Budget coming up in October. However, once delivered, we will be within touching distance of the 3% deficit target and the days of massive Budget adjustments will be behind us.'[4] This view was echoed a few weeks later by Taoiseach Enda Kenny when he was reported as saying, 'This is not going to be an easy budget . . . we hope that this will be the last difficult budget.'[5]

These reassuring comments from Enda Kenny and Michael Noonan echo those made in 2009 by the late Brian Lenihan. But they fly in the face of evidence that Official Ireland's Plan A – compliance with the wishes of the Troika – is simply not working.

ECONOMIC GROWTH UNDER PLAN A

Every year, when the Minister for Finance presents the budget for the following year, he also forecasts the government's finances for several years. This requires annual economic growth forecasts for that period so that estimates of tax revenue and government spending can be prepared. By examining successive downward revisions in the growth forecasts by the Department of Finance, we can see the shrivelling of Ireland's growth prospects.

Consider the expectations for national economic output for 2012. In particular, consider Ireland's real GDP. In December 2009 it was expected that 2012 would see real GDP growth of 4.5 per cent.[6] In each of the following budgets, the growth expectation for 2012 was reduced further. By December 2012, when the year was almost complete, expected growth for the year had been reduced to just 0.9 per cent.[7] Six months after the year-end, the Central Statistics Office (CSO) computed that real GDP growth had actually amounted to only 0.2 per cent in 2012.[8] This has been the persistent pattern for expected economic growth since 2008. Steady growth is forecast for the medium term. But as the medium term approaches and becomes the short term, growth forecasts must be revised downwards to face the reality of weak to barely noticeable economic growth (see Figure 1.1).

Figure 1.1: Growth Estimates Have Had to Be Repeatedly Revised Downwards

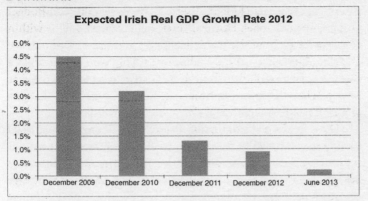

Source: Data derived by author from budgetary documentation published by the Department of Finance: http://www.finance.gov.ie.

If the economic forecast included in his budget speech by Brian Lenihan in December 2009 had come to fruition, Ireland's nominal GDP would reach €205 billion by 2014. But applying July 2013 Central Bank forecasts (for 2013 and 2014) to the actual GDP figures recorded by the CSO (for 2009–12) indicates that Ireland's nominal GDP is likely to reach only €172 billion by 2014 (see Figure 1.2).

Figure 1.2: Disappointing Economic Growth Has Led to an Ever-Widening Gap between Where Annual Economic Output Should Be and Where It Has Ended Up

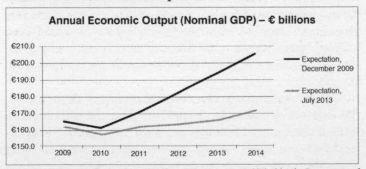

Source: Data derived by author from budgetary documentation published by the Department of Finance: http://www.finance.gov.ie.

In other words, our current estimate of national output for 2014 is 16 per cent below what Brian Lenihan anticipated at the end of 2009. That is equivalent to over €7,000 for every man, woman and child living in the State. Imagine how much better things would be if that missing growth had materialised.

Note that nominal GDP is the measure favoured by Official Ireland to estimate Ireland's economic capacity. As we will see later, this measure has severe shortcomings as it includes the profits of foreign multinationals over which Ireland has little real claim. However, even by this measure, Ireland's economic growth looks largely stagnant and its capacity to service its debts looks weak.

Ireland appears trapped in a low- or no-growth world. Yet, in reaction to the absence of meaningful economic growth, Official Ireland is declaring victory for Plan A. In July 2013 Michael Noonan asserted that 'Difficult decisions have been taken and these have helped re-position our economy on a more sustainable, export-led growth path. These difficult decisions are now beginning to bear fruit, as evidenced by two successive years of modest growth.'[9] But real growth in 2012 was just 0.2 per cent, with the same expected for 2013 (estimates will be published by the CSO in March 2014).

DEBT AND DEFICIT UNDER PLAN A

In his December 2010 budget speech, Brian Lenihan stated, 'This Budget is the first instalment of the National Recovery Plan. The Plan plots a course to sustainability for our country: sustainable public finances, sustainable public services, sustainable growth, and sustainable employment.'[10] The budgetary adjustments pushed through by successive Irish governments have been breathtaking in their extent. Between 2008 and 2013, adjustments totalling over €30 billion have been pushed through. And we still have additional adjustments to make.

In April 2013 Lenihan's successor as Minister for Finance Michael Noonan reiterated the government's commitment to confronting Ireland's debt and its deficit when he said: 'The Irish financial crisis could be summarised in one word: debt – national debt and personal debt. The Government is committed to dealing with both national and personal debt.'[11] However, reduced economic growth and the increased cost of the bank bailout have pushed Ireland's debt far beyond what was originally projected (see Figure 1.3). By July 2013, it was anticipated that Ireland's 2014 debt level would reach €210 billion rather than the €166 billion expected back in late 2009.

Figure 1.3: Ireland's Public Debt Levels Have Had to Be Continually Revised Upwards

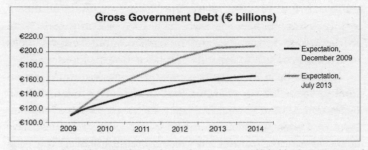

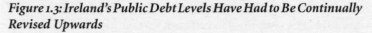

Source: Data derived by author from budgetary documentation published by the Department of Finance: http://www.finance.gov.ie.

An examination of Ireland's government deficit (the annual gap between government spending and revenue) from 2009 to 2014 shows a better picture. Some slippage was expected in 2013 and 2014 but, broadly speaking, Ireland showed considerable success in reducing its government deficit, despite the large shortfall in economic growth (see Figure 1.4).

Figure 1.4: Ireland's Government Deficits Have Been Substantially within Target

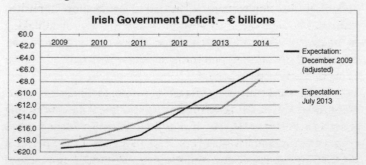

Source: Data derived by author from budgetary documentation published by the Department of Finance: http://www.finance.gov.ie.

However, it must be remembered that Ireland's 2014 deficit will be reduced by €2 billion as a result of interest rate concessions made by the Troika in September 2011.[12] In February 2013 concessions were made in relation to the promissory notes.[13] Promissory notes are a form of IOU, which the Irish government used instead of cash to invest additional monies into Anglo-Irish Bank in 2009 and 2010. The cost of this investment and the annual €3.1 billion interest charge on these notes later became matters of major political controversy. In February 2013, the promissory notes were restructured and the annual interest burden significantly reduced.

Ireland is unable to meet its original deficit target even with a very substantial annual Troika contribution. Ireland's 2013 gross government deficit was expected, back in December 2009, to equal €9.5 billion. As of July 2013, it is expected to be €12.5 billion. Without those Troika interest concessions, it would have been €14.5 billion. Whatever way you examine the figures, Ireland still has a huge gap between government spending and government revenue.

This raises the fundamental question of whether Ireland's debts are on a sustainable trajectory. The Fiscal Advisory Council thinks they are. In April 2013 it concluded in its assessment report: 'The debt ratio is expected to peak this year at 121.1 per cent of GDP, with small declines over the following two years. By 2015, the debt ratio is envisaged to be declining at a rate of 4.1 percentage points of GDP.' But it did warn of 'the fragility of debt sustainability over the medium-term' and estimated a 'one-in-four chance of the debt to GDP ratio failing to stabilise by the end of the projection period' without further policy measures beyond those currently planned.[14]

In June 2013, the IMF warned that 'if real GDP growth was to stagnate at 1 per cent per year in the medium term, debt . . . would be on an unsustainable path to 136 per cent of GDP by 2021.'[15] But CSO figures show real GDP growth of just 0.2 per cent in 2012. And official November 2013 figures estimate the same rate of real growth for 2013. At this rate of economic growth, Ireland's debts simply don't look sustainable.

THE BANKS UNDER PLAN A

The bitter prospects for Irish banking were set out in a December 2010 letter to the Troika from then Minister for Finance Brian Lenihan and Central Bank Governor Patrick Honohan. They wrote that 'A fundamental downsizing and reorganisation of our banking system is essential.'[16] That is Plan A for the Irish banking system. Since 2010, Irish banks have sent out the message that they're 'open for business'. But this message is utterly contradicted by the sharp drop in Irish loan volumes envisaged under Plan A. On top of that, the Irish economy must cope with foreign banks – such as HBOS (formerly Halifax Bank of Scotland), Ulster Bank and Danske Bank – reducing their lending or exiting retail banking altogether.

By June 2013, loans advanced to Irish households had dropped by 31 per cent from their 2008 peak, while loans advanced to Irish companies had dropped by 52 per cent from their peak.[17] The sharp reduction in bank credit has put huge strain on Irish businesses as they struggle to reduce bank loans at a time of falling profits. One experienced accountant wrote: 'Liquidity doesn't exist in Irish business. It has been drained out of working capital cycles to pay loans that cannot be paid from profit.'[18] The consequence of liquidity being drained from the wider economy at a time of reduced profits and incomes is a spiralling level of problem loans.

In April 2013 the then head of supervision at the Central Bank Fiona Muldoon stated that half of all loans to small and medium firms were non-performing.[19] Meanwhile, the proportion of mortgage loans in financial distress (i.e. which are either in arrears or have already been restructured) was 29 per cent for owner–occupiers and 47 per cent for buy-to-let landlords in September 2013.[20] The large proportion of loans in distress forced Irish banks into making ever larger provisions for bad debts and loan write-offs. Alarmingly, Irish banks were loss-making in 2012[21] even before they made any fresh provisions for bad debts.

As it was the perilous state of its banks which triggered Ireland's financial crisis, the Troika understandably wished to re-examine the banks' finances before Ireland exited its programme. So the

Irish government agreed that bank stress tests – aimed at gauging banks' resilience to economic shocks – scheduled for Europe in early 2014 would be brought forward in Ireland to late 2013. Minister for Finance Michael Noonan publicly stated that he did not expect that these stress tests would require banks to find extra capital to meet their regulatory requirements.[22] Given that the stress tests would be carried out under the aegis of the Central Bank, it is unclear how Minister Noonan squared his comments with Article 107 of the Maastricht Treaty: 'governments of the Member States undertake ... not to seek to influence the members of the decision-making bodies of the ECB or of the national central banks in the performance of their tasks.'[23]

Minister Noonan's anticipation of the results of tests which had yet to commence indicates the authorities' acute sensitivity on this matter. Bad and all as Ireland's budgetary mathematics and estimates of debt sustainability may be right now, they would be immeasurably worse if substantial additional funds were required by Ireland's banks. A look at the detailed financial statements of Ireland's main banks might give even Michael Noonan pause for thought. Buried within the 2012 financial statements of Allied Irish Banks (AIB) (414 pages long), Bank of Ireland (381 pages long) and Permanent TSB (187 pages long) are two sets of values for each bank's loan books. The first is the book value – this shows the value at which the bank is carrying its loans on its balance sheet (net of the money set aside to cover potential losses on loans) on the assumption that the loans will be held until they mature. The second set of figures shows the fair value – this is the bank's estimate of the amount at which the loans could be bought or sold in a transaction today between willing parties, i.e. it is the bank's estimate of the loans' current commercial value. These two sets of figures for Ireland's main banks as of December 2012 are set out in Table 1.1.

Table 1.1: The Banks' Own Fair Value Estimates of Their Loans Fell Far Short of Their Official Book Value

31 December 2012 €billion	Book Value	Fair (Commercial) Value	Gap
AIB	€73.0	€64.1	-€8.9
BOI	€92.6	€80.4	-€12.2
PTSB	€31.8	€24.3	-€7.5
	€197.4	€168.8	-€28.6

Source: Figures extracted by author from the 2012 financial statements of AIB, Bank of Ireland and Permanent TSB.

So, the Irish banks' estimates of the fair value of their loans amounted to €28.6 billion less than their combined book value. Interestingly, this gap is very close to one commentator's estimate that Ireland's banks require an extra €30 billion in capital.[24] Plan A doesn't seem to be working very well for Ireland's banks.

HUMAN SUFFERING UNDER PLAN A

Long-term unemployment exacts tremendous social and economic tolls. International research shows that, for an individual, a prolonged period out of work leads to reduced lifetime earnings (up to 20 per cent in some cases), higher probability of future unemployment (up to 2.3 times that of the average), and a deterioration in the creativity and competencies that he or she can contribute to the workplace.

As of September 2013, there were officially 282,900 unemployed,[25] an official unemployment rate of 13 per cent. But if we add to the ranks of the unemployed those receiving disability allowance, disablement benefit, illness benefit and the invalidity pension, as well all those undergoing activation measures to get them back into work (e.g. Back to Education courses), the total without work in Ireland exceeds 600,000 people. This means that 28.5 per cent, or over one quarter, of the workforce is without work (see Table 1.2).

Table 1.2: **The Real Number of Those Out of Work Is Almost 600,000**

Category	Number		Date
Unemployed	**282,900**	13.0%	September 2013
Disability allowance	101,784	4.8%	December 2012
Disablement benefit	14,202	0.7%	December 2012
Invalidity pension	50,053	2.3%	December 2012
Illness benefit	64,429	3.0%	December 2012
	513,368	23.7%	
Activation measures	86,042	4.0%	March 2013
	599,410	**27.7%**	

Source: Data derived from Department of Social Protection (2012), Statistical Information on Social Welfare 2012, available from: http://www.welfare.ie, accessed January 2014; and Michael Hennigan (2013), 'Irish Economy 2013: Unofficial rate of employment remains over 20%', 10 June, available from: http://www.finfacts.ie, accessed January 2014.

This frighteningly high figure exists even with the high volume of emigration, without which the number of people out of work would be even higher. Two hundred thousand more people emigrated in the period 2008–12 than in the period 2002–7.[26] So the number of those left unemployed by the financial crisis could be as high as 800,000.

Those still with a job are not safe from suffering. Falling incomes and falling property prices have led to a collapse in personal wealth for most and mortgage arrears for many. The Central Bank managed to represent the March 2013 mortgage arrears figure as being just 12 per cent of total mortgages by (a) ignoring mortgages in arrears for less than three months; (b) ignoring buy-to-let mortgages; (c) ignoring mortgages that have already been restructured; and (d) looking at the number of loans in arrears rather than the amount owed on those loans. Taking these factors into account, in terms of mortgage loan balances, the actual proportion in arrears in November 2013 was 33 per cent, almost three times the figure released by the Central Bank.

In the face of this growing human distress, government ministers continue to valiantly champion Plan A. But the public seems to be growing tired of it and of them. An opinion poll taken in November 2013 showed that, since the February 2011 general election, the government parties had lost over one quarter of their aggregate support.[27]

PLAN A ISN'T WORKING...

If Plan A is struggling in Ireland, there is a similar story across the remainder of the eurozone periphery. In July 2013 the IMF published its Selected Issues Paper following its recent consultation on the euro area.[28] A graph buried on page 52 of that report shows that, since 2008, economy-wide debt levels (as measured by total debt to GDP ratios) have continued to grow relative to national income across the eurozone periphery. Debt levels have grown even though the financial crisis is a debt crisis and even though the principal objective of public policy across the periphery is to reduce debt (see Figure 1.5).

Figure 1.5: Across the Eurozone, Total Debt Has Risen (and Not Fallen) since 2008

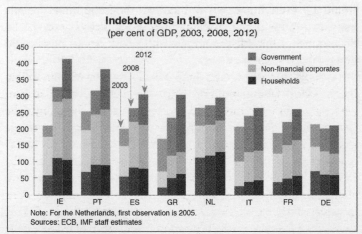

Source: IMF (2013), 'Euro Area Policies', Selected Issues Paper, July, available from: http://www.imf. org, accessed January 2014.

The rise in the debt-to-GDP ratios above can be attributed either to overall debt levels rising or to GDP levels falling (which has been the case in Greece and some other countries). The growth in economy-wide debt in the case of Greece is alarming as that country had its debts significantly restructured in the period surveyed. It's also notable that the situations in Italy and in France are quietly but steadily deteriorating.

But it's the situation in Ireland that is most alarming. Far from being the cleverest boy in the eurozone class, Ireland has the highest debt level and has experienced the largest growth in economy-wide debt since 2008. Whether it is judged in terms of economic growth, the number out of work, the number emigrating or the number experiencing mortgage loan distress, it is clear that Plan A is not working. Even in terms of its own core objective – to bring Ireland's debt outlook to a sustainable level – Plan A is not working.

Yet, Official Ireland clings to Plan A, evoking the lesson in Hillaire Belloc's poem 'Jim': 'and always keep a hold of nurse, for fear of finding something worse.' The most astonishing aspect of Plan A is that, despite its palpable economic failure, it faces no corresponding political failure. Nobody likes Plan A. Everyone grumbles about it. And political parties forced to implement it find that they inevitably lose popular support. Yet, despite its obvious and deep unpopularity, no mainstream political force appears to have a viable and clear-cut alternative to Plan A. But there is an alternative. And it offers the prospects of higher economic growth, lower emigration and a more sustainable future for Ireland and its people. This book presents that alternative. This is Plan B.

02 BOOM

Lenin was certainly right. There is no subtler, no surer means of overturning the existing basis of society than to debauch the currency. The process engages all the hidden forces of economic law on the side of destruction, and does it in a manner which not one man in a million is able to diagnose.

John Maynard Keynes

THE LONG GOODBYE TO BRITAIN

The independent Irish State has seen civil war, a European war, economic boom, economic bust, and many political and policy changes. But one political objective has remained constant since before the State was even founded: a loosening of Ireland's ties with Britain. Governments come and governments go. Political coalitions of varying composition are formed. But, since the First Dáil was formed in 1919, every Irish government has sought to loosen Ireland's political and economic dependency on Britain.

The Proclamation of the 1916 insurgents made clear the burning desire to escape from Britain's shadow:

In the name of God and of the dead generations from which she receives her old tradition of nationhood, Ireland, through us, summons her children to her flag and strikes for her freedom.... We declare the right of the people of Ireland to the ownership of Ireland, and to the unfettered control of Irish destinies, to be sovereign and indefeasible. The long usurpation of that right by a foreign people and government has not extinguished the right, nor can it ever be extinguished except by the destruction of the Irish people. In every generation the Irish people have asserted their

right to national freedom and sovereignty: six times during the
past three hundred years they have asserted it in arms....[1]

The assertion of the Irish people's right to national freedom and
sovereignty didn't finish with the end of the War of Independence
or with the conclusion of the Anglo-Irish Treaty on 6 December
1921. It continued thereafter.

From implementing major institutional change to changing
the colour of the post boxes, between 1922 and 1932 the first
Cumann na nGaedheal-led government attempted to Gaelicise
the nation. That government was followed by Eamon de Valera's
Fianna Fáil-led administration, which systematically ran down the
constitutional infrastructure inherited from the Treaty. Later de
Valera-instituted changes were even more significant in allowing
Ireland to escape from British influence. The 1937 Constitution
replaced the office of Governor-General, the King's representative
in Ireland appointed after consultation with London, with that of
democratically elected President. And, following a short but bitter
trade war with Britain, sparked by the Irish government's refusal to
pay land annuities, Ireland got back the Treaty Ports in 1938. These
were three Irish naval facilities (at Spike Island and Berehaven in
County Cork and at Lough Swilly in County Donegal) that Britain
had retained after 1921. Getting back the Treaty Ports meant that
Ireland's decision to opt for neutrality in World War II was all the
more dramatic an assertion of national sovereignty. The decision
to remain neutral was also part of Ireland's long goodbye to Britain.
And it was followed in September 1948 by the Fine Gael Taoiseach
John A. Costello's announcement that Ireland would leave the
British Commonwealth and declare herself a republic.

The government's decision in 1972 to join the European
Economic Community (EEC), the forerunner of the EU, was
couched in terms of escaping Britain's influence. Then Taoiseach
Jack Lynch stated: '... by remaining outside the EEC we would
be also increasing our dependence on Britain. Can any Irishman
seriously want this?'[2]

Rarely, if ever, have our politicians stated that there could be
circumstances where it might be in Ireland's interests to increase

our dependence on Britain. Rather, it has always been taken as self-evident that increased dependence on Britain is, of itself, a bad thing for Ireland.

Ireland's 1979 decision to join the EEC's Exchange Rate Mechanism (ERM) was to trigger a break between the Irish currency – the punt – and sterling. Since independence, Ireland had had its own currency. But the Irish authorities had long maintained a fixed exchange rate of parity or 1:1 with sterling. By opting in 1979 to tie the Irish currency to a basket of European currencies of which sterling was not a member, Ireland exited this arrangement. A Dáil debate on this decision saw anti-British sentiment reach absurd levels as the leader of the Irish Labour Party opposed a policy promoting cheap food:

> *This attitude by the British is becoming a tiresome and repetitive matter which will doubtlessly go on whatever the political persuasion of any British Government. Their particular version of a cheap food policy is, I fear, one of the hangovers of Britain's colonial past and it will be a particularly difficult one to change.*[3]

Even after the 1998 Good Friday Agreement and the British Queen's 2011 visit to Ireland, the anti-British reflex in Irish politics runs deep.

In July 2013 there was a discussion on Irish television about the recent decision by the eight largest developed world countries (G8) to clamp down on legal tax avoidance. Hearings in the British House of Commons into some of the more arcane corporate tax strategies used for tax avoidance were also discussed. A Labour Party TD stated: 'It's all centred around an agenda to criticise our corporation tax rate. That's the whole point of why they're doing it.' He was backed up a Fianna Fáil senator who stated:

> *This is being driven by the British parliament, British MPs, and I won't take any lectures from the UK and nor should Ireland by the way…. So why are they doing this? They're doing it to undermine us.*[4]

The fact that, at a time of global pressure on national budgets, other countries might have good reason to increase their tax revenues did not influence the opinion of the senator. Rather, the muscle memory of ancestral antagonism kicked in to inform us that the British were doing this 'to undermine us'.

THE LONG HELLO TO EUROPE

Just as Ireland followed a steady course away from British influence over the last century, the countries of Western Europe have been drawing closer together since 1945 and the calamity of World War II. The geopolitical contrast between 1945, the final year of World War II, and 1914, the first year of World War I, could hardly have been greater. In 1914, the European powers of Britain, Germany and France were among the most powerful in the world, while the United States lurked across the Atlantic Ocean. By 1945, Britain was financially exhausted; Germany had been militarily destroyed before being geographically truncated, then divided; France was humiliated; and Western Europe, reeling in the wake of two world wars, was an economic wasteland politically dominated by two external powers – the United States in the west and, in the east, the Soviet Union. This was a sharp comedown for the imperial powers of 1914. Once masters of the world, by 1945 they were reduced to dependents whose political fate would be decided by others. Weak economic performance in the decades thereafter, in contrast to the rise of emerging nations in Asia and South America, merely underlined this point.

The foundation for the European Union was laid in 1951 with the establishment of the European Coal and Steel Community (ECSC). At that point, France lacked the economic muscle to assert itself while West Germany lacked the diplomatic muscle. However, together, the two states had both economic and diplomatic power. On top of that, it was intended that the supranational ideals of their alliance would replace the nationalistic ideals of the nineteenth century, which had done Europe so much damage in the first half of the twentieth century. In the words of Jean Monnet, arguably the chief architect of what would become the EU:

The sovereign nations of the past can no longer solve the problems of the present: they cannot ensure their own progress or control their own future. And the Community itself is only a stage on the way to the organised world of tomorrow.[5]

This practical alliance was garnished with idealism about the common destiny of all Europeans; 'the ever closer union of the peoples of Europe' was explicitly stated in the first line of the preamble to the 1957 Treaty of Rome,[6] which established the EEC. At first there were just six EEC member states: France, West Germany, Italy and the three Benelux countries. They were joined in 1973 by Ireland, Britain and Denmark. Greece joined in 1981; Portugal and Spain in 1986. In 1990, after the fall of the Iron Curtain, the former East Germany became part of the EEC as part of a reunited Germany. In 1995, Austria, Finland and Sweden joined. In 2004, the community saw its biggest enlargement to date when Cyprus, the Czech Republic, Estonia, Hungary, Latvia, Lithuania, Malta, Poland, Slovakia and Slovenia joined. In 2007, Romania and Bulgaria became members. And in 2013, Croatia brought the EU's membership up to 28.

Meanwhile, the EEC had become the European Community (under the 1992 Maastricht Treaty) and the European Union (under the 2009 Lisbon Treaty). In 1985, the Schengen Agreement saw the creation of open borders without passport controls between most member states. In 1986, the EU began to use its own flag, and the Single European Act, which foresaw the creation of a single market by 1992, was signed. In 2012 the EU even received the Nobel Peace Prize for having 'contributed to the advancement of peace and reconciliation, democracy, and human rights in Europe.'[7]

Ireland took part enthusiastically in every stage of deeper European integration. There was no Irish counterpart of the stream of euro scepticism which permeated British politics. And, in Dublin, there was bafflement when, in 2013, the British Prime Minister David Cameron promised his people an in–out referendum on EU membership. In Ireland, anti-British sentiment had been sublimated into a reflexive habit of enlightened support for the EU. This helped Ireland to sleepwalk into membership of the euro.

IRELAND'S DECISION TO JOIN THE EURO

It was the Maastricht Treaty of 1992 that committed Ireland to membership of European Economic and Monetary Union (EMU) and to eventually adopting the euro as its currency. The Dáil debate on the matter in May of that year reflected the twin drivers of a reflex reaction against what Britain was doing (it had won a treaty opt-out regarding adoption of the new currency) and instinctive pro-Europeanism (in eagerly agreeing to sacrifice the punt on the altar of the new euro). Taoiseach Albert Reynolds set out the reason for joining EMU:

> EMU *is the natural extension of the Single Market. Increased co-ordination of economic policies and the development of a single monetary policy and a single currency under European Monetary Union are required, if the full benefits of the Single Market are to be realised.*[8]

Minister for Energy Bobby Molloy justified the decision in terms of escaping from the malign influence of Britain:

> *Formerly we were too dominated by Britain and our inevitable colonial links with that country. Changes in the British sterling rate automatically affected prices in Ireland and our very economic welfare, but we were not consulted about these changes. We had no such right. We were simply aggrieved bystanders. That is why I simply cannot accept the argument of those critics of European Community membership who claim that Irish sovereignty has been diminished as a consequence of our membership. Nothing could be further from the truth.*[9]

Former Taoiseach Garret FitzGerald, who was probably the Dáil's most avid pro-European, regretted that the debate had got 'bogged down in the irrelevant issue of abortion and in the economic issues of grants and all the rest.'[10] Worryingly, no speech in this debate asked the appropriate fundamental questions: did EMU meet the conditions for a functioning currency union and did it make economic sense for Ireland to join it? This failure by the

Dáil to comprehend what was going on reflected the wider situation across the EU. One Dutch central banker commented, 'Not one of the politicians who agreed the Maastricht Treaty understood what they were doing.'[11] This lament was confirmed by one of those who had signed the treaty, British Foreign Secretary Douglas Hurd. He quipped, 'Now we've signed it – we had better read it.'[12]

WHAT MAKES A CURRENCY ZONE WORK, OR NOT WORK?

Having had a currency arrangement with Britain that worked smoothly, Irish governments tended to take currency arrangements for granted. But economists devote considerable attention to the question of what makes a common currency zone work or – to put it in their terms – what constitutes an Optimum Currency Area (OCA). An OCA is defined as a geographical region in which it would maximise economic efficiency to share a single currency. Clearly it makes sense that different parts of Ireland should share a common currency. But does it make economic sense for the entire continent of Europe to share one? Nobel Prize winner Robert Mundell is the leading academic theorist in this area. Based on his work, the four often-cited criteria for a successful currency union are:

1. Labour mobility across the region. This includes physical ability to travel, lack of cultural barriers to free movement (such as different languages) and institutional arrangements.

2. Capital mobility and price and wage flexibility across the region.

3. A risk-sharing system, such as an automatic fiscal transfer mechanism to redistribute money to areas within the region that are in short-term economic difficulty.

4. Participant countries should have similar business cycles. Should countries in a currency union have business cycles that are not synchronised, setting an interest rate appropriate to the entire region would be all but impossible for the Central Bank.[13]

Using these criteria, comparing Ireland's old currency arrangement with sterling to the present arrangement under the euro is a good illustration of OCA theory. First, let's take labour mobility.

Labour Mobility

The freedom for labour to move exists under both arrangements. But, in practice, there is much more human traffic across the Irish Sea than between Ireland and mainland Europe. It is notable that, after substantial net emigration returned to Ireland after 2008, jobless young Irish people have been far more likely to travel to Britain, the US, Australia or Canada, where they might face visa difficulties, than to mainland Europe, where they would face none.

Capital Mobility and Wage Flexibility

In theory there are capital mobility and price and wage flexibility across the eurozone. But, in practice, there is little wage flexibility. Huge divergences in wage costs developed across the eurozone from 1997 onwards. With little internal migration taking place, there was no immediate counterweight to these divergences. This contrasted with the situation under Ireland's old currency arrangement with sterling, since Irish and British capital and labour markets were (and still are) substantially integrated.

Automatic Fiscal Transfers

There was no automatic fiscal transfer system under Ireland's old currency arrangement. And there isn't one under its new arrangement either. European regional aid could be considered by some to be a fiscal transfer mechanism, but it aims to balance out long-term differences in income across the EU rather than short-term differences in national business cycles. So it doesn't count.

Similar Business Cycles

And whereas Ireland and Britain have had similar business cycles, with economic peaks and troughs occurring at similar times, the same cannot be said for the eurozone. In the late 1990s, Ireland's economy was booming while Germany was struggling to cope with the cost of national reunification a decade earlier.

Ireland's old currency arrangement with sterling had three of the four criteria for a successful currency zone, while the arrangement Ireland entered into in 1992 had none (see Table 2.1).

Table 2.1: Effects of Parity with Sterling in Contrast to those of Euro Membership

	Old: Parity with Sterling	New: Euro Membership
Labour mobility	Yes	Not really
Economic flexibility	Yes	Not really
Fiscal transfers	No	Not really
Similar business cycles	Yes	No

There were plenty of warnings of the dangers of establishing EMU. Nobel laureate and monetarist Milton Friedman stated, 'The Euro has been motivated by politics, not economics'[14] and that it was 'highly unlikely [the euro] is going to be a great success'.[15] The more left-wing Keynesian Franco Modigliani warned of the difficulties 'in a system which will have fixed exchange rates' and of the need for 'a great deal of flexibility in the behaviour of wages of individual countries, [each] having differential productivity growth and facing external shocks'.[16] Former EU Commissioner Ralf Dahrendorf warned in 1995 that 'the currency union is a great mistake and a risky, reckless and misguided goal that will divide Europe rather than unite it.'[17]

A JP Morgan study in May 2012 examined the suitability of various possible combinations of states for a currency union and concluded that, because its range of economic divergence was very large, EMU was particularly unsuitable.[18] Monetary unions based on a reconstitution of the Ottoman Empire or on all countries on the planet beginning with the letter 'M' are, in the estimation of that study, better suited to monetary union than the major countries of the eurozone (see Figure 2.1).

Figure 2.1: The Countries of the World Beginning with the Letter 'M' Are More Suitable for Monetary Union than the Major Countries of the Eurozone

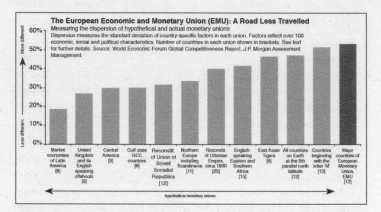

Source: JP Morgan (2012), 'Eye on the Market', 2 May, available from: http://www.ssherman associates.com, accessed January 2014, p. 1.

INTEREST RATES IN THE BOOM

The first signal that things were going to be different for Ireland inside the eurozone was that Irish interest rates dropped sharply. This happened in anticipation of high Irish interest rates being replaced by much lower eurozone interest rates that would be heavily influenced by the needs of Germany, which was coping economically with the effects of national reunification. Interest rates that might have been right for the eurozone as a whole were far too low for Ireland's national circumstances. This spawned Ireland's credit bubble; its debt bubble; its property bubble; its employment bubble; its cost bubble (relative to our international competitors); and a public spending bubble. The effect of this was outlined in a 2005 note by Rossa White of Davy Stockbrokers:

> But losing control over monetary policy to Frankfurt in 1999 has had an impact on the Irish economy. Think of record house

building, annual credit growth running at 25%, a near doubling in house prices, and 5.5% average inflation in the service sector. While potentially storing up problems for the future, interest rate-sensitive sectors of the economy contributed handsomely to three years of above-trend growth, followed by a strong recovery from a shallow recession. All of which poses the important question: at what level would the key policy rate stand if the Central Bank of Ireland still had control over it?[19]

In answering the question he had thus posed, White estimated that, as of early 2005, 'an appropriate policy rate for Ireland is around 6 per cent, fully four percentage points above its actual level.' He went on to warn:

There is no doubt that an inappropriate policy rate for Ireland is fuelling the booming residential construction sector. One way to think about it is to imagine the mayhem that would ensue were interest rates to rise to 6%. Our worry is that an elongated boom could lead to a more severe correction in the housing market when rates finally begin their ascent (to 3% rather than 6%) or when sentiment changes.[20]

Cheap credit was the single greatest cause of Ireland's credit and property booms. This is illustrated in Figure 2.2, which appeared in a November 2008 paper published by John Taylor, the developer of the Taylor Rule, used to estimate the appropriate central bank policy rate for an economy. Taylor's graph shows clearly that the greater the degree of interest rate reduction a country got from eurozone membership (mapped on the horizontal axis), the greater the increase in housing investment in that country (vertical axis) (see Figure 2.2).

Figure 2.2: *The Greater the Interest Reduction Conferred by Eurozone Membership, the Greater the Increase in Construction Activity*

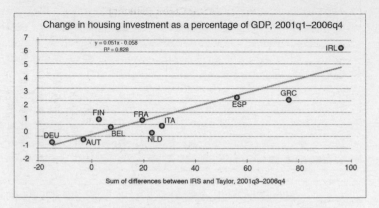

Source: John Taylor (2008), 'The Financial Crisis and the Policy Responses: An Empirical Analysis of What Went Wrong', November, available from: http://www.stanford.edu/~johntayl/FCPR.pdf, accessed January 2014.

Is it pure coincidence that the three outliers at the top right of Figure 2.2 – Ireland, Greece and Spain – are among the countries now suffering the greatest financial distress in the eurozone crisis?

CREDIT IN THE BOOM

The direct result of overly cheap credit was that borrowing levels took off. As then Taoiseach Albert Reynolds said in the Dáil debate to ratify the Maastricht Treaty in May 1992, 'Our interest rate differential vis-à-vis the Deutsche-Mark has been reduced from 9 per cent to less than 1 per cent.'[21] Between 1992 and 2008, the volume of credit advanced to the Irish private sector grew from €27 billion to €395 billion (see Figure 2.3). This was a staggering increase which fundamentally distorted property prices, economic activity levels and wages.

Figure 2.3: Irish Private Sector Credit Volumes Ballooned Once High Irish Interest Rates Converged on Lower Eurozone Rates

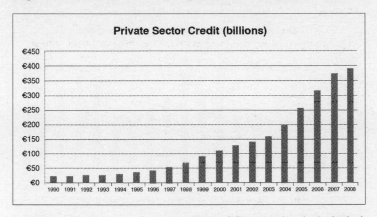

Source: Data extracted by author from various editions of The Statistical Yearbook of Ireland, *available from: http://www.cso.ie, accessed January 2014.*

Between 1992 and 2008 the Irish private sector experienced astonishingly high growth rates that were well ahead of the underlying rates of economic growth. While Figure 2.3, depicting total private sector credit, appears to show an exponential rise in debt levels from the early 1990s onwards, Figure 2.4, which illustrates annual growth in credit, shows a somewhat different picture. It shows that there were two periods of exceptionally high credit growth (the late 1990s and the mid-noughties), with an intervening period of credit growth slowdown in the early noughties that coincided with a global economic slowdown. Indeed, there was a considerably higher rate of private sector credit growth over the five years 1995–2000 than over the five years 2002–7 (see Figure 2.4).

Figure 2.4: The Boom in Irish Credit Did Not Begin in the 2000s – It Began in the 1990s

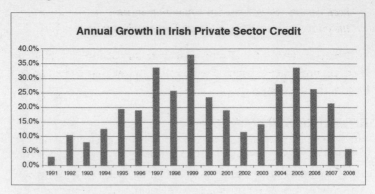

Source: Data extracted by author from various editions of The Statistical Yearbook of Ireland, available from: http://www.cso.ie, accessed January 2014.

This pattern suggests that Ireland's debt bubble did not begin in the early noughties; in fact it had begun much earlier and had merely slowed down during the 2001–2 global economic downturn before accelerating once more. This perspective is reinforced when we examine a news report from 30 April 1999:

> Fine Gael's Finance spokesman has said that the government would be well advised to take serious note of the statement by the Governor of the Central Bank. Michael Noonan said that, while inflation is not a serious threat to the economy, astronomical house prices in Dublin are. In a statement, he said that false markets do not last.
>
> The Governor of the Central Bank has warned the country's mortgage lenders that they are advancing too much money to borrowers. In a letter to executives of commercial banks and building societies, Maurice O'Connell said that routine inspections had revealed disturbing practices by the commercial institutions in assessing the size of loans.
>
> Mr. O'Connell said that there was evidence that the excessive rise in house prices had been partly driven by the ready availability of mortgage finance on generous terms. The fact that this letter was addressed to the chairman of every mortgage lender in the country

underlines the seriousness with which the Central Bank is addressing this issue. Maurice O'Connell says in the letter that the bank has been concerned for some time now that institutions are breaching the guidelines governing amounts that people can borrow.[22]

It is clear that interest rates that were inappropriately low for Irish circumstances spawned a boom in credit that began as far back as the mid-1990s.

HOUSE PRICES IN THE BOOM

The impact of rampant credit growth was felt most immediately in Ireland's property market. Over the course of 15 years, and especially after 1996, Ireland saw astonishing house price increases. While house prices took off across the country, the phenomenon was concentrated in Dublin (the wealthiest part of the country) and among second-hand houses (which tended to be situated in central locations, whereas many new properties were built on the edges of major conurbations). Second-hand house prices peaked in Dublin in 2006 and in the rest of the country in 2007. By 2006, the prices of Dublin's second-hand houses had increased to nearly five times their 1996 values (see Figure 2.5).

Figure 2.5: Fuelled by Cheap Credit, Irish House Prices Took Off in the Mid-1990s

Source: Data extracted from housing statistics of the Department of Environment, Community and Local Government, available from: http://www.environ.ie, accessed January 2014.

The price increases for other property categories and for the country as a whole looked relatively modest by comparison to the astonishing rises in Dublin (see Table 2.2).

Table 2.2: Property Price Rises in Dublin and Nationally

Category	Price rise 1996 – peak	Annualised Increase
Dublin – second hand	+391%	+19%
National – second hand	+341%	+17%
Dublin – new	+329%	+16%
National – new	+270%	+15%

Source: Data extracted from housing statistics of the Department of Environment, Community and Local Government, available from: http://www.environ.ie, accessed January 2014.

It is clear from Figure 2.5 that there was an inflection point in the trend of Irish house prices in the mid-1990s. Prior to that, house price rises had been modest and steady in pace. After that, rises were large and rapid. The timing of this inflection further calls into question the notion that things only began to go off the rails in the noughties. Figure 2.5 shows that it was in the mid-1990s that the trend line of Irish house prices fundamentally changed, as Ireland's membership of EMU became increasingly certain and as our interest rates converged downwards to German levels. With cheap credit and rampant house price increases, property investment became a one-way bet. Eventually, in 2008, prices reversed across all categories. This was the first year since 1987, 21 years earlier, that Irish house prices had fallen.

EMPLOYMENT AND COSTS IN THE BOOM

When I graduated from University College Dublin in 1981 with a B.Comm degree, Ireland was pushing all the right buttons to attract jobs. There was national consensus behind the efforts to attract foreign employers into Ireland. The Industrial Development Authority (IDA) was offering much larger capital grants to employers than is now permitted under tightened-up EU rules. And Ireland didn't just offer such mobile capital a 12.5 per cent corporation tax rate – we offered them a 0 per cent corporation tax rate.[23] But despite Ireland's aggressive pursuit of employment projects, overall job creation remained modest. Most of my B.Comm classmates emigrated. Then, in the mid-1990s, there was a clear inflection point in the graph of the number employed in Ireland,[24] after which Ireland experienced rampant jobs growth (see Figure 2.6).

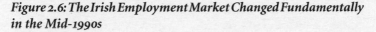

Figure 2.6: The Irish Employment Market Changed Fundamentally in the Mid-1990s

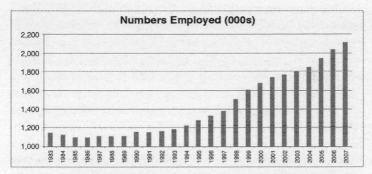

Source: Data extracted by author from various editions of The Statistical Yearbook of Ireland, available from: http://www.cso.ie, accessed January 2014.

Initially, more jobs were available for those who wished to remain in Ireland. Later, the jobs growth facilitated people who, having previously emigrated, wished to return to Ireland. And then, in the noughties, tens of thousands of immigrants came to Ireland to fill job vacancies (see Figure 2.7).

Figure 2.7: Annual Immigration Grew Steadily from 1991 to 2006

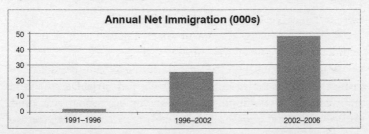

Source: Data extracted by author from various editions of The Statistical Yearbook of Ireland, available from: http://www.cso.ie, accessed January 2014.

If you flew into Dublin Airport during this period, you might
have seen a prominently positioned IDA Ireland poster. This
featured young, attractive and smart-looking people against the
background of a large new factory. You could have easily got the
impression that the roots of Ireland's 'Celtic Tiger' phenomenon
lay in a successful shift from an inward-looking and backward
economy to an outward-looking and modern one that was rooted
in state-of-the-art industry.

You would have been wrong. A sectoral analysis of Ireland's
jobs growth from 1998 onwards shows that the highest rates of
employment growth were experienced by the interest rate sensitive
sectors. With interest rates inappropriately low, those sectors
most exposed to the resulting credit bubble – construction and
financial services – experienced the greatest jobs boost (see Figure
2.8). Overall, the number of people employed in industry actually
declined.

*Figure 2.8: The Jobs Miracle Was Strongest in the Interest Rate
Sensitive Sectors of Construction and Financial Services*

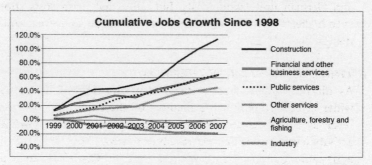

Source: *Data extracted by author from various editions of* The Statistical Yearbook of Ireland,
available from: http://www.cso.ie, accessed January 2014.

Why did jobs in Irish industry decline over this period? A key
reason is that industry is the economic sector most exposed to
international competition. And, from the late 1990s until 2008,
the cost of Irish labour exploded relative to our international
competition. For example, relative to Germany, Ireland experienced
a 58 per cent rise in unit labour costs over 13 years (see Figure 2.9).

Figure 2.9: Irish Unit Labour Costs Diverged from Germany's from 1999 Onwards

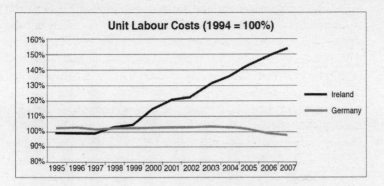

Source: *Organisation for Economic Cooperation and Development (OECD) total economy unit labour cost data, available from: http://stats.oecd.org, accessed January 2014.*

Again, we can see a clear inflection point around the late 1990s as the prospect of inappropriately low interest rates became ever clearer. Prior to 1998–9, there was no marked divergence in Irish and German unit labour costs. But, after that, Irish costs shot ever higher while German costs were contained and even sank marginally.

THE PUBLIC SECTOR IN THE BOOM

As ultra-low interest rates spawned a property boom and a wider economic boom, the finances of the Irish public sector received a massive boost. Rising employment and economic activity levels meant that tax revenues soared. Between 1997 and 2007 annual government revenue grew from €23 billion to €60 billion, increasing at an annual pace of 10 per cent (see Figure 2.10). Ireland's public finances weren't just receiving a boost from more people working, earning higher incomes and paying more in taxes; as more people who had been unemployed were able to return to the workforce, the government no longer needed to pay social welfare to so many.

Figure 2.10: Despite Substantial Tax Cuts, the State Enjoyed Huge Revenue Increases

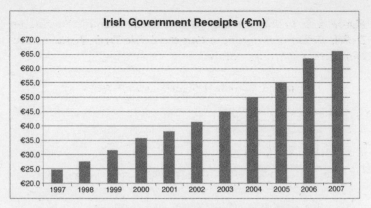

Irish Government Receipts (€m)

Source: Data extracted from housing statistics of the Department of Environment, Community and Local Government, available from: http://www.environ.ie, accessed January 2014.

All this permitted the Irish government to have the best of both worlds: it was able to reduce tax rates and to significantly increase government spending. Government spending more than doubled over the decade 1997–2007, having grown at an annual pace of 8.5 per cent. The conventional hard choice of governing politicians – whether to increase spending or introduce tax cuts – simply did not face the Irish government.

IRELAND'S ACCOUNT WITH THE REST OF THE WORLD

During the boom decade 1997–2007 there was at least one economic warning sign: our trading account with the rest of the world steadily deteriorated. A country's current account balance measures whether it is increasing the net amount the rest of the world owes it (when it runs a surplus) or increasing the net amount it owes the rest of the world (when it runs a deficit). The main driver of the current account balance is the balance of trade, i.e. net revenue from exports minus payments for imports. The boom years saw Ireland's current account balance slip gradually from healthy surplus to significant deficit (see Figure 2.11). This slippage should have given the lie to any notion that Ireland's boom was

largely export driven – if that had been the case, our surplus would
have held steady or even grown.

*Figure 2.11: Ireland's Swing from Current Account Surplus to
Deficit Belied the Argument that the Celtic Tiger Rested on the
Foundation of Strong Exports*

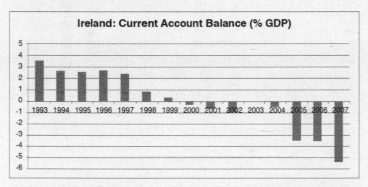

Source: OECD *balance of payments data, available from: http://stats.oecd.org, accessed January
2014.*

Instead, it seemed that Ireland's boom was overly reliant on
domestic consumption and insufficiently based on exports.

THE WATCHDOGS IN THE BOOM

As all these imbalances were building, where were the
watchdogs? Surely they must have seen what was happening? And
surely they must have issued warnings? Sadly, the watchdogs failed
to bark. Some whimpered, but none so loud that anyone would
notice. Some, like the Irish Central Bank, barked back around the
turn of the century but, as ever-rising house prices appeared to
contradict their warnings, they became quieter lest people think
they were, well, barking. Others saw that Irish property prices and
construction investment were at perilously high levels but failed
to anticipate that a collapse in the construction industry would
cause a collapse in the Irish banking system, which would affect
the entire economy.

After the crash, a report stated that the Department of Finance
'had warned the [2002–7] government about the dangers of the

economic policy it was following, but that its advice was overruled by the Cabinet'.[25] This report was based on the Wright Report, which was commissioned by the Department. It certainly fits with the popular belief that the dogs in the street knew something was wrong and that then Taoiseach Bertie Ahern wilfully ignored official advice as he drove the economy over a cliff. But is it true? It is telling that not a single direct quote from any departmental document was offered in support of the report's central conclusion. Instead, the report lamely asserts, 'There are examples of where such advice was tendered in writing. We have also been advised of some important oral briefs that reinforced the Department's concern about pro-cyclicality. But these are not part of the official record.'[26] How can they not be part of the official record? Why not reprint this written advice? And why not tell us who orally warned whom of what and when?

As a special advisor to the 2002–7 government, I had access to cabinet agendas, memoranda and documentation. I cannot ever recall seeing a written Department of Finance warning to the Cabinet. Having issued several private warnings in vain, I was avidly searching for institutional allies to argue that Ireland was in a bubble. Instead I can recall departmental messages which were consistently reassuring. If one examines published departmental documents from the time, one sees no indication that the Department of Finance saw what was coming. Consider its *Economic Review and Outlook*, published in August 2005, which included the following:

> *The outlook for the Irish economy is one of growth, [but] there are significant downside risks which could alter this picture. The key risks in the scenario presented in this review are:*
>
> *   *The possibility of a sharp dollar correction leading to an appreciation in the euro. This risk has not receded despite the recent fall in the value of the euro.*
>
> *   *Persistent high oil prices which could pose a serious threat to Irish growth and prices.*
>
> *   *Eurozone growth, which is already low, could turn out to be lower.*

- *The pace at which new housing output adjusts downwards to more sustainable levels, given that sector's importance in terms of real growth in the economy.*[27]

Note that this was not a warning but, rather, a generic list of risk factors which might cause the Department's baseline forecast to undershoot. This is the kind of statement that would typically accompany any set of financial projections. Its aim was not to warn so much as to insulate those who prepared the projections from subsequent criticism when, as one would expect, subsequent deviations emerged. Note also that, in its statement of risk factors, the government department with responsibility for banking failed to list the Irish banking system as a potential risk.

In 2005, the Economic and Social Research Institute (ESRI) prepared its *Medium Term Review*, which looked forward to the period 2005–12. This review concluded that 'The fundamental factors driving the Irish economy remain quite favourable.' And while the document did point to the unsustainable overdependence on construction activity, it failed to make the connection between a nosedive in Ireland's construction industry and a nosedive in its banking sector. The lowest annual rate of Gross National Product (GNP) growth in the review's 'Low Growth Scenario' was +2.7 per cent in 2009. As it turned out, Ireland's GNP, or the total value of economic output produced by the citizens of the country, dropped by 9.1 per cent that year.

The IMF also failed to see the dangerous connection between Ireland's construction and banking sectors when it reported on Ireland in May 2006:

Economic performance remains strong, assisted by good policies. However, growth has become heavily reliant on building investment and competitiveness has eroded. The share of the construction sector in GDP is high and likely to fall over the next few years.[28]

Three months later, in August 2006, the IMF underlined its complacency regarding Ireland's banking system:

The Irish financial sector has continued to perform well since …
2000. Financial soundness and market indicators are generally
very strong. The outlook for the financial system is positive.[29]

The Organisation for Economic Cooperation and Development
(OECD) fared little better in analysing the situation in Ireland and
in predicting what would happen in the Irish economy. It reported
in its *Economic Survey* in November 2006:

Ireland has continued its exemplary economic performance,
attaining some of the highest growth rates in the OECD…. Further
progress will require strong productivity growth and continued
increases in labour supply.[30]

The body formally charged with maintaining the stability of
Ireland's financial system, the Irish Central Bank, presented its
annual *Financial Stability Report* on 14 November 2007. By that time,
the share price of Ireland's leading bank, Bank of Ireland, had already
lost nearly one half of its peak value.[31] The share prices of other, more
vulnerable, banks had fallen even further (see Figure 2.12).

Figure 2.12: In November 2007 the Irish Central Bank Issued a
Reassuring Report on the Stability of Ireland's Banks Despite a 50
per cent Share Price Drop in Bank of Ireland

Source: http://www.FTmoney.com, accessed August 2013.

Despite the ominous message that should have been conveyed by the sharp fall in Irish bank share prices and despite its own earlier warnings at the start of the decade, the Central Bank came to a wholly complacent – and wrong – conclusion about the Irish banking sector:

> *The Irish banking system continues to be well-placed to withstand adverse economic and sectoral developments in the short to medium term.*[32]

Another body that has won considerable influence over policymaking in Ireland is the EU, particularly its Directorate General for Economic and Financial Affairs (DG ECFIN). This body also failed to diagnose what was happening in Ireland. On 3 March 2008 it published its *Macro Fiscal Assessment of Ireland.* The EU's conclusion gave no indication of the crisis that lay just around the corner:

> *Despite the weakening in the budgetary position in 2007, the medium-term objective, which is a balanced position in structural terms, was reached by a large margin.*[33]

When this report was written, the Director-General of the DG ECFIN was Klaus Regling. Despite having failed in 2008 to diagnose that Ireland was in a bubble or to predict that Ireland faced a bust, Regling was asked in 2010 by the Irish government to investigate the origins of 'the crisis in the banking system in Ireland'. He later went on to head up the European Stability Mechanism (ESM) and, in that position, to give Ireland lectures as to how it should conduct itself.

The clear evidence, when one examines their public statements at the time, is that the economic watchdogs failed to bark. They didn't appear to notice that Ireland was in a bubble. And they didn't warn that Ireland faced a bust. It is ironic that some of the institutions that have gained the most influence over Irish official policymaking since the bust – the Department of Finance, the IMF, the Irish Central Bank and the EU – signally failed to anticipate it. But have these bodies seen a consequent reduction in their influence on policymaking here? No. In a spectacular example of moral hazard, they have seen their influence over policy in Ireland grow dramatically.

It may seem that I am holding these economic watchdogs to a standard I failed to reach myself. After all, I was a special advisor to Minister for Justice, Equality and Law Reform Michael McDowell during the 2002–7 government. Am I not partially responsible for the unconstrained build-up of the economic bubble over those years? I would offer the following four points as an answer to that question. First, the problems in the Irish economy resulted largely from our membership of the euro rather than from domestic errors, although there were many of these. The international dimension of this crisis is evident from the simultaneous debt crises that have erupted across the eurozone periphery. Second, with the independence of Ireland's Central Bank enshrined in EU treaty law, elected Irish policy-makers had only limited authority in the critical areas of monetary policy and financial regulation. Third, in the key area where elected Irish policy-makers did have authority – government spending deficits – prudence was exercised and structural surpluses were run. It was only after 2008 that international bodies changed the way structural surpluses were calculated to conclude that during the latter years of the boom Ireland had actually been running structural deficits. After the fact, these bodies were wise. But they delivered no warnings in real time. Finally, and critically, I did argue that the economic boom up to 2007 was due to inappropriately cheap eurozone credit. Using a pseudonym, I wrote the following in the April/May 2005 edition of *Magill* magazine:

> *The elephant in the room that our conventional economists ignore is the role played by the permanently low interest rate regime we enjoy, courtesy of the European Monetary Union (EMU). Since 1 January 1999, we have enjoyed interest rates more suited to depression-ridden Germany. The result has been a boom in credit, a bubble in house prices and almost a doubling in annual employment growth with a focus on the interest-sensitive sectors*

of our economy such as construction (employment up 63% since 1998) and financial services (employment up 38%). Employment in manufacturing has actually declined since 1998.

Where is all this leading? Simple. We can't keep increasing our borrowings forever. The constraint on our indebtedness will not be interest rates as in previous decades. It will be our debt capacity. We risk maxing out on debt and thereby making ourselves vulnerable to any short-term economic set-back. The closest parallel may prove to be the Japanese economy. They too experienced a growth miracle built on a credit bubble induced by politically-determined interest rates. Their bubble was pricked in 1991. If their experience is anything to go by, the bursting of the Irish bubble would be a nightmare. The economy would prove impervious to monetary and fiscal stimulus, as individuals and corporations sought to curtail spending in order to reduce their bank borrowings. A downward spiral of asset prices, forced liquidations and further falls in asset prices could result. Growth would prove elusive and the financial sector would be in permanent crisis.

If my words of warning gained little traction, that is hardly surprising. You don't make yourself popular by going around a party telling people that the more they drink now the worse their headaches will be later. Furthermore, even though some may consider me an economist, I lack any formal economic qualification. Why would people pay attention to a chartered accountant giving economic warnings when the formal economic watchdogs were issuing reassuring commentaries?

WHY DID THE WATCHDOGS FAIL?
Across the board, professional economists in respected institutions failed to comprehend and to warn of what was going on. It may not suit those professional economists to admit that today. It may be easier to shelter behind the myth that Bertie blew it than to admit that they didn't see the bust coming. But why did the watchdogs fail? Across the world, central bankers and regulators made serious intellectual mistakes. As the former head of the US Central Bank, or Federal Reserve, Paul Volcker, wrote:

I am afraid we collectively lost sight of the importance of banks and markets that would robustly be able to maintain efficient and orderly functioning in time of stress. Nor has market discipline alone restrained episodes of unsustainable exuberance before the point of crisis. Too often, we were victims of theorizing that markets and institutions could and would take care of themselves.[34]

In Ireland, central bankers and regulators displayed moral failings as well as intellectual ones. We have seen how the Irish Central Bank issued warnings about growing dangers in 2000. But, after those dangers had gotten considerably worse, the same institution issued reassuring noises in 2007. In part, this represented intellectual insecurity and the institutional fear of perennially crying 'wolf' only for no danger to emerge.

However, even when the authorities had knowledge of wrongdoing within a financial institution, they did little. Consider a report into Irish Nationwide Building Society prepared by Scott J. Dobbie, distinguished British banking expert. He reported a failure by the Financial Regulator to act, even when in possession of disturbing information.

The Financial Regulator, from the documentation I have seen, appears to have understood and delineated the critical INBS issues well before they caused trouble, but equally failed fully to use its powers under the [Building Societies] Act by pursuing these issues, being apparently mollified by bland assurances from the INBS Chairman and CEO.[35]

But perhaps the greatest error on the part of the watchdogs was the failure to comprehend how membership of the eurozone fundamentally changed the dynamics of the Irish economy. Previously Ireland had followed British interest rates. Because of the similarity and degree of integration of the two economies, an interest rate policy that was broadly right for Britain was usually broadly right for Ireland. Now, as a member of the common-currency area, Ireland got eurozone interest rates. But, because of the Irish economy's dissimilarity to and lack of integration with

the rest of the eurozone, an interest rate policy that was right for
the eurozone was usually wrong for Ireland. With the punt gone
and with Ireland locked into the euro, this changed everything.

To understand the fundamental change brought about by
Ireland's membership of the eurozone, consider the sequence of
economic forces that were unleashed in Ireland by a decade of
interest rates that were too low (see Figure 2.13).

*Figure 2.13: The Sequence of Economic Forces Unleashed in
Ireland by Low Interest Rates*

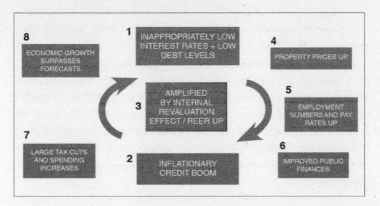

1. Eurozone interest rates were too low for Ireland's needs at a time
    when, with low starting debt levels, Ireland had considerable
    capacity to take on additional debt.

2. Inappropriately low interest rates spawned an inflationary
    credit boom.

3. With a freely floating national currency, all of these inflationary
    factors should have led to a rise in the currency value and an
    external revaluation of asset values and costs. But because we
    were locked into the euro, these inflationary pressures fed into
    an internal revaluation through increased inflation – especially
    of property prices and wage costs – and increased economic
    activity. This led to an increase in Ireland's real effective
    exchange rate ('REER').

4. This inflationary credit boom increased the value of property assets, causing sharp rises in people's wealth.

5. An increase in property values spawned an increase in construction activity, which spilled over into the general economy, leading to increases in pay and in the number employed.

6. This increased tax revenues for the government and reduced the number drawing welfare, causing an improvement in the public finances.

7. This permitted increased public spending and reduced taxes.

8. Economic growth rates were consistently higher than expected.

The nature of the economic game had changed fundamentally for Ireland for the decade 1997–2007. Rather than trying to interpret and comprehend this profound change, Official Ireland preferred to luxuriate in self-congratulation.

Ireland's boom-time prosperity was not built on the sustainable foundations of enduring national advantage. It was built on the shaky foundations of a reversible credit boom, which was about to go bust.

BUST

Panics do not destroy capital; they merely reveal the extent to which it has been destroyed by its betrayal into hopelessly unproductive works.

John Mills, 'On Credit Cycles and the Origin of Commercial Panics'

BOOM TURNS TO BUST – THE TRIGGER

By 2006 Irish house prices had experienced nearly two decades of almost uninterrupted rises. This triggered a high and growing degree of complacency in Ireland that property was 'a safe investment' with little risk of price falls.

In fact, if people had paid attention to one financial theorist they might have drawn the opposite conclusion. Hyman Minsky (1919–96) argued that capitalist financial systems have an inbuilt proclivity to financial instability. His financial instability hypothesis can be summarised by the phrase 'Success breeds success, which breeds failure', or 'Success breeds excess, which breeds failure.'

By 2006, the 'success' of continually rising Irish property prices had certainly bred excess. Davy Chief Economist Rossa White issued a warning in March of that year.

The frenzy in the Irish property market has intensified. In the last six months, house price inflation has re-accelerated to an annualised rate of 15%. In the Dublin market, prices are now rising at an annualised 20% lick, up from only 3% less than a year ago. But rents have only recently recovered after a three year period in which they were in decline. As a result, yields have been driven down to unprecedented depths. Something does not feel right.[1]

White made specific reference to the widespread belief that
desirable properties in Dublin's prosperous inner suburbs would
always hold their value. However, he noted that it was in precisely
these locations that prices had reached their 'craziest'. He went
through the financial mathematics facing a prospective buy-to-let
landlord, or investor, who was considering entering the market in
2006. And he issued a clear warning:

> *Investors must be extremely bullish about rental growth in order to
> justify the sort of record valuations ascribed to residential property
> in central Dublin. To us, this looks like boundless optimism.
> Supply in Dublin is set to remain plentiful for the next couple of
> years as we continue to build houses at a rate four times quicker
> than the European average. Meanwhile, interest rates will rise by
> at least one percentage point over the next year, pushing investors'
> break-even point lower and lower. The amount of cash sloshing
> around due to SSIAs and tax cuts, and the current buoyancy of the
> housing market, suggest that valuations will become even more
> stretched over the next 18 months. But the fundamentals suggest
> that it will be an adjustment in prices – rather than rents – that
> will eventually bring valuations down to more realistic levels.*[2]

Rossa White's warning wasn't generally heeded and it didn't
get the resonance it deserved. A year and a half later, in September
2007, Professor Morgan Kelly of UCD achieved far more resonance
with a piece he wrote for the *Irish Times*. He explained why, in his
opinion, optimistic expectations for 'a soft landing' in the property
market were unlikely to be realised.

> *With lending rates based on five-year euro swaps now risen to over
> 6.5 per cent and rental yields fallen to 4 per cent, new investors
> cannot cover interest from rent and are entirely reliant on capital
> gains from rising prices. With commercial property prices slowing
> rapidly, and loans taken out a few years ago needing to be rolled
> over, there is a strong risk of a sudden exodus from the market and
> a collapse in prices.*[3]

With interest rates considerably higher than rent yields,[4] landlords faced a cash squeeze. For this meant they would have had to pay out more in interest expense than they were taking in in rental income. They would only have been willing to use cash savings to sustain this situation as long they thought that future capital gains would make it worth their while. But, as prices started to fall, the prospect of capital gains evaporated and the logic of attempting to rapidly dispose of the investment property began to take over.

Kelly's warning earned him considerable renown. However, it provoked a rebuke from Taoiseach Bertie Ahern, who lashed out in a speech, saying, 'Sitting on the side-lines, cribbing and moaning is a lost opportunity. I don't know how people who engage in that don't commit suicide because frankly the only thing that motivates me is being able to actively change something.' But Kelly and his warning were about to be richly vindicated.

HOW ECONOMIC BUSTS UNFOLD

The problem for Ireland now was that, having made a huge bet on property prices continuing to rise, those prices were now falling sharply. Media discussion focussed on the slowdown in the economy and many people understandably blamed the banks for the predicament which Ireland now found itself in. But the collapse in economic activity was due to much more than just the failure of the banks. Ireland was experiencing the cold turkey effects of exiting a decade-long economic bubble. The resulting collapse in private sector wealth brought on by falling property prices was central to Ireland's financial and economic crisis. This had unleashed a balance sheet recession.

The term balance sheet recession (BSR) was devised by Japanese economist Richard Koo to describe the crisis afflicting his country since 1990. Koo explained the dynamics of a BSR in a 2011 paper.

When a debt-financed bubble bursts, asset prices collapse while liabilities remain, leaving millions of private sector balance sheets under water. In order to regain their financial health and credit ratings, households and businesses are forced to repair their balance sheets by increasing savings or paying down debt. This act of deleveraging reduces aggregate demand and throws the economy into a very special type of recession.[5]

One key problem of a BSR is that falling asset prices damage people's financial health and they then save more in an attempt to regain it. While increased saving may make sense from the perspective of the individual, when it is attempted by a whole society it leads to falling demand. This then puts further downward pressure on asset prices, thereby reinforcing the whole pernicious phenomenon.

A second key problem of a BSR is that conventional central bank policy to stimulate an economy in a recession – interest rate cuts – won't be very effective. Instead of reacting to interest rate cuts by spending more, people with damaged balance sheets will use the proceeds of the cuts to reduce their debt rather than to increase their spending. Nor, according to Koo, is there any reason to believe that bringing back inflation will work, because people are paying down debt in response to a fall in asset prices, not changes in consumer prices. Koo issued a stark warning of the deflationary spiral that can result when people continue to try to save under these circumstances:

> *When the private sector deleverages in spite of zero interest rates, the economy enters a deflationary spiral because, in the absence of people borrowing and spending money, the economy continuously loses demand equal to the sum of savings and net debt repayments. This process will continue until either private sector balance sheets are repaired or the private sector has become too poor to save (i.e. the economy enters a depression).*[6]

The economic conditions which Ireland now faced were described nearly 80 years ago by Professor Irving Fisher when he used his theory of debt deflation to explain the Great Depression in the US. According to Fisher:

> *At some point of time a state of over-indebtedness exists. This will tend to lead to liquidation, through the alarm either of debtors*

or creditors or both. Then we may deduce the following chain of consequences in nine links:

1. *Debt liquidation leads to distress selling and to*
2. *Contraction of deposit currency, as bank loans are paid off, and to a slowing down of velocity of circulation. This contraction of deposits and of their velocity, precipitated by distress selling, causes*
3. *A fall in the level of prices, in other words, a swelling of the dollar. Assuming, as above stated, that this fall of prices is not interfered with by reflation or otherwise, there must be*
4. *A still greater fall in the net worths of business, precipitating bankruptcies and*
5. *A like fall in profits, which in a 'capitalistic', that is, a private-profit society, leads the concerns which are running at a loss to make*
6. *A reduction in output, in trade and in employment of labor. These losses, bankruptcies and unemployment, lead to*
7. *Pessimism and loss of confidence, which in turn lead to*
8. *Hoarding and slowing down still more the velocity of circulation.*

The above eight changes cause

9. *Complicated disturbances in the rates of interest, in particular, a fall in the nominal, or money, rates and a rise in the real, or commodity, rates of interest.*[7]

Every single one of Fisher's conditions exists in Ireland today (see Table 3.1).

Table 3.1: Every Single One of Fisher's Debt-Deflation Conditions Exists in Ireland Today

Fisher Debt-Deflation Condition	Status in Ireland
1. Over-indebtedness	Yes
2. Distress selling	Yes – but stemmed by NAMA* and by bank forbearance on mortgage arrears
3. Contraction of deposit currency	Yes – money supply trending down since 2007
4. Fall in level of prices	Significant fall in asset prices. No fall in consumer prices
5. Greater fall in net worth of businesses	Yes – ISEQ index of Irish stocks still down 60% from peak
6. Fall in profits	Yes
7. Reduction in output	Yes – GDP and GNP sharply down
8. Hoarding	Yes – savings rate up sharply
9. Rise in real interest rates	Yes. As a result of very low inflation, real interest rates have risen even though nominal interest rates remain low

National Asset Management Agency

A large government deficit is the economic remedy proposed by Richard Koo for a balance sheet recession. Koo argues that when the private sector is aggressively saving, the public sector must do the opposite to facilitate this. Therefore, the public sector must run large deficits if economic activity levels are not to shrink to the point where a depression is triggered.

> *Every several decades, the private sector loses its self-control in a bubble and sustains heavy financial injuries when the bubble bursts. That forces the private sector to pay down debt in spite of zero interest rates, triggering a deflationary spiral. At such times and at such times only, the government must borrow and spend the private sector's excess savings, not only because monetary*

policy is impotent at such times but also because the government
cannot tell the private sector not to repair its balance sheet.[8]

Running large government deficits (i.e. a loose fiscal policy)
is a key element in the economic strategies of the US and Britain
in countering the post-2008 economic downturn. However, apart
from the Troika (EU, ECB and IMF), nobody seemed willing to lend
to the Irish government. Coupled with that, the Troika insisted
on sharp fiscal contraction, a policy that aimed to reduce the
government deficit. Koo warned specifically against the economic
measures which the Irish government was forced into.

Although anyone can push for fiscal consolidation in the form of
higher taxes and lower spending, whether such efforts actually
succeed in reducing the budget deficit is another matter entirely.
When the private sector is both willing and able to borrow
money, fiscal consolidation efforts by the government will lead to
a smaller deficit and higher growth as resources are released to
the more efficient private sector. But when the financial health
of the private sector is so impaired that it is forced to deleverage
even with interest rates at zero, a premature withdrawal of fiscal
stimulus will both increase the deficit and weaken the economy.[9]

Irving Fisher came to a similar conclusion in the 1930s. *The*
Economist magazine explained his remedy in a 2009 article:

What is the solution? Fisher wrote that it was 'always economically
possible to stop or prevent such a depression simply by reflating
the price level up to the average level at which outstanding
debts were contracted.' Alas, reflation is not so simple. Although
stabilising nominal home prices would help short-circuit the debt-
deflation dynamics now under way, any effort to maintain them
at unrealistically high levels (where they still are in many cities)
is likely to fail. Higher inflation could help bring down real home
prices while allowing nominal home prices to stabilise, and reduce
real debt burdens.[10]

Reflating price levels through aggressive quantitative easing (i.e. a loose monetary policy) is the other key element in the economic strategies of the governments of the US and Britain in countering the post-2008 economic downturn. But, with Irish monetary policy controlled from Frankfurt and directed to the needs of a continent rather than a single country, this has not been possible in Ireland.

INTEREST RATES IN THE BOOM

Real interest rates measure the difference between interest rates and inflation. As a consequence of being locked into the euro, Ireland got interest rates that were quite inappropriate to its national needs. Thus, in the boom year of 2003, Ireland's average mortgage interest rate was less than the inflation rate, meaning Ireland's real interest rate was negative.[11] But, as Ireland tipped into its deepest recession for several generations, real interest rates rose from below 2 per cent to over 5 per cent.

Figure 3.1: Perversely, Real Interest Rates Rose as Economic Depression Beckoned

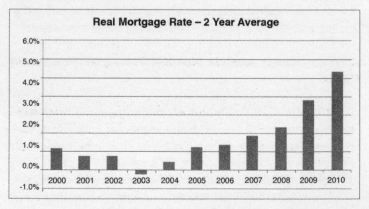

Source: *Author's calculations based on CSO data.*

A rise in real interest rates was one of the conditions Fisher identified with the phenomenon of debt deflation. In Figure 3.1, we can see this illustrated in the case of Ireland.

The Taylor Rule, which economists use to identify the appropriate central bank interest rate for different countries, illustrates what had happened. The rule uses two variables, a country's inflation rate and its amount of spare economic capacity, to determine a country's appropriate interest rate. The Taylor Rule suggests that the higher a country's inflation rate, the higher its interest rate should be. The rule also indicates that higher spare economic capacity (as evidenced, for example, by higher levels of unemployment) should trigger lower interest rates. In the boom years, up to and including 2007, Ireland had higher inflation than the eurozone average. On that account, it needed a higher interest rate than the eurozone average. In those years it also suffered a greater scarcity of spare economic capacity with, for example, a much lower unemployment rate. On that account, too, it needed a higher interest rate than the eurozone average. Around 2008, the situation relative to the eurozone flipped. Irish inflation went from being above the eurozone average to being below it, so Ireland now required an interest rate *below* the eurozone average. With a massive rise in unemployment, scarcity of spare economic capacity also fell below the eurozone average; on this account, too, Ireland now required an interest rate *below* the eurozone average (see Table 3.2).

Table 3.2: Around 2008, the Situation Relative to the Eurozone Flipped

	Ireland 1997–2007	Ireland 2008
Inflation	Above EZ average	Below EZ average
Scarcity of spare economic capacity	Above EZ average	Below EZ average
Eurozone interest rate	**Too low for Ireland**	**Too high for Ireland**

This switch in Ireland's circumstances came in 2008, when Irish households and companies had become massively over-indebted following a decade-long debt binge. So at the worst possible time for

Ireland, eurozone interest rates shifted from being inappropriately low for Ireland to being inappropriately high.

HOW THE EURO CHANGED THINGS IN THE BUST
Just as the economic Establishment had failed to grasp the effects of Ireland's membership of the eurozone on the boom, it also failed to comprehend how it affected things in the bust. To understand the fundamental change brought about by Ireland's membership of the eurozone, consider the sequence of deflationary effects after 2008 (see Figure 3.2).

Figure 3.2: The Sequence of Deflationary Effects after 2008

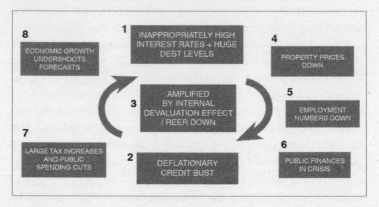

1. Eurozone interest rates became too high for Ireland's needs, at a time when our elevated debt levels needed to be reduced.

2. Inappropriately high interest rates and the aftermath of a deflating credit bubble unleashed a deflationary credit bust.

3. With a freely floating national currency, these deflationary impulses would have been expected to lead to a fall in the currency value and 'an external devaluation' of asset values and costs. But, since Ireland is locked into the euro, these deflationary pressures fed into 'an internal devaluation' through deflation, especially of property prices and wage costs, and decreased economic activity. This led to a decrease in Ireland's real effective exchange rate ('REER').

4. This led to a sharp fall in the value of property assets, causing a sharp drop in people's wealth.

5. This impacted on the general economy in the form of a decrease in retail and services activities and a significant drop in the number employed.

6. It led to a sharp fall in tax revenues for the government and an increase in the number drawing welfare, causing a catastrophic deterioration in the public finances.

7. This led to both public spending cuts and increased taxes.

8. Since 2007, Ireland's annual economic growth rate has consistently come in below that forecasted. And forecasts of future economic growth have had to be repeatedly revised downwards.

The boom/inflationary cycle of Ireland's euro membership lasted at least a decade. It remains to be seen how long the bust/deflationary phase endures.

ADDITIONAL WOE: IRELAND'S FOREIGN EXCHANGE RATE

Normally, a country that is experiencing a deep recession will see its currency drop compared to other currencies. This brings depressed economies two advantages: first, currency devaluation makes the country's exports more competitive; and, second, by making imports more expensive, it increases domestic demand for goods produced at home. But, even though it suffered a once-in-a-century recession that started in 2008, Ireland's currency rose rather than fell (see Figure 3.3).

Figure 3.3: Instead of Financial Crisis Leading to Devaluation, Ireland's Currency Rose Sharply against Sterling

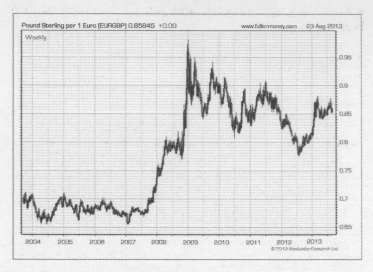

Source: *http://www.FTmoney.com, accessed August 2013.*

In the years running up to 2008, €1 averaged £0.67–£0.68 sterling in value. But, in the years after 2008, it averaged over £0.85. This represented a currency appreciation by the euro in excess of 25 per cent, which made life considerably more difficult for Irish manufacturers attempting to export into Britain or competing with British companies exporting into Ireland. It also made holidays in Ireland expensive for tourists from the sterling area.

Back in the days when Ireland still had its own currency, the punt, exporters would become alarmed if the punt rose above parity with sterling. Applying the euro currency shifts to the punt, with €1 worth £0.85 sterling as of August 2013, the old punt would have been worth £1.08 sterling. At its peak, when the euro reached £0.98 sterling in early 2009, the old punt would have been worth £1.24 sterling. But few noticed these excruciating currency moves. The punt had long been abolished and with it disappeared any significant attention to currency moves against sterling in Irish public debate.

THE COLLAPSE IN PROPERTY PRICES

House prices peaked in Dublin in 2006 and, for the country as a whole, they peaked the following year.[12] A rapid descent soon began (see Figure 3.4).

Figure 3.4: What Goes Up Must Come Down?

Source: Data extracted from housing statistics of the Department of Environment, Community and Local Government, available from: http://environ.ie, accessed January 2014.

By the end of 2012, house prices had fallen by about one third from peak, according to official statistics,[13] but there were significant variations in the rate of fall across different property categories (see Table 3.3).

Table 3.3: Variations in the Rate of House Price Fall across Different Property Categories

Category	Price Fall 2007–2012	Annualised Fall
Dublin – second hand	-35%	-8.3%
National – second hand	-35%	-8.3%
Dublin – new	-45%	-11.2%
National – new	-33%	-7.6%

Source: Author's calculations, based on Department of Environment, Community and Local Government statistics.

Having experienced the highest percentage rise in the boom, Dublin properties now experienced the greatest fall in the bust.

But there were those who asserted that even larger house price falls had taken place. Dermot O'Leary, Chief Economist at Goodbody Stockbrokers, pointed to much lower property price levels at auctions compared to those noted by the official statistics.

In a report based on Allsop Space auctions released this morning, we estimate a 68% decline from the peak.[14]

The decline in commercial property values was even more pronounced than that implied for residential property by official indicators. By the end of 2012, the Jones Lang LaSalle index of Irish commercial property indicated a fall of 67 per cent from its 2007 peak.[15]

THE COLLAPSE IN WEALTH

Having spent a decade loading up on property investments, many Irish people felt the heavy losses in wealth brought about by the sharp fall in property prices after 2007. The Central Bank estimated that, by March 2013, Irish households had suffered a wealth hit of the order of €250 billion from peak levels (see Figure 3.5).[16]

Figure 3.5: Ireland's Net Wealth Peaked in Early 2007 Before Commencing a Long Decline

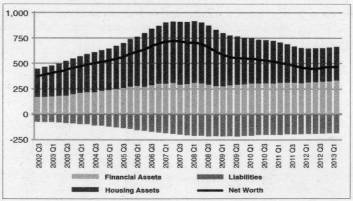

Source: Central Bank (2013), Quarterly Financial Accounts, Q1, *available from: http://www. centralbank.ie, accessed January 2014.*

The vast bulk of this wealth loss had occurred following house price drops, which the Central Bank reckoned were close to 50 per cent. But if one used a house price drop of 60 per cent, the wealth loss would have been a staggering €330 billion. This larger figure amounts to 2.5 times annual national income or GNP.

As Ireland's property wealth was shrivelling, much public debate was taken up with trying to persuade citizens that economic growth of 2 or 3 per cent was possible or that a growth of 10 per cent in exports should be welcomed. Of course such developments should be welcomed. But improvements in Ireland's ongoing economic performance of a few per cent here or there can't compensate for a collapse in the value of our accumulated savings that may range from 200 to 250 per cent of annual income. Yes, our profit and loss account might be improving; but our balance sheet has been crushed. This is a balance sheet crisis about stupendous liabilities and falling asset values even more than it is a crisis about income levels.

A sharp rise in the national savings rate (i.e. the proportion of disposable income which citizens save) was one very direct result of the tattered state of Irish household balance sheets. Household savings rose from around 9 per cent of disposable income before 2008 to around 13–14 per cent afterwards (see Figure 3.6).

Figure 3.6: The Wealth Collapse Led to Sharply Increased Savings

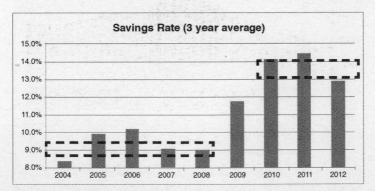

Source: Author's calculations based on Eurostat data.

Governing politicians liked to imagine that this increased rate of saving was a precautionary reaction to the annual uncertainty of what each national budget would bring. But it is far more likely that increased savings were a natural reaction to the damage family balance sheets had suffered. It was the attempt to repair balance sheets, rather than uncertainty over the national budget, that was the main driver of increased personal savings.

THE COLLAPSE IN DOMESTIC DEMAND

Ireland's membership of the euro now unleashed a perfect storm on Ireland's economy and its people. By 2008, the worm had turned. From then on, interest rates were too high for Ireland, the value of the euro was too high for Ireland and property prices were too high for Ireland. The resulting fall in property prices and collapsing wealth levels added to deflationary pressures, which led to a collapse in domestic demand.

Ireland's economy has become a tale of two economies. The export sector, after stumbling in 2008 and 2009, has now recovered and grown to record its highest activity level ever. But, as of mid-2013, domestic demand levels continued to contract, albeit at a much slower pace than in 2008 and 2009 (see Figure 3.7).

Figure 3.7: A Tale of Two Economies: Booming Exports and a Stagnant Domestic Economy

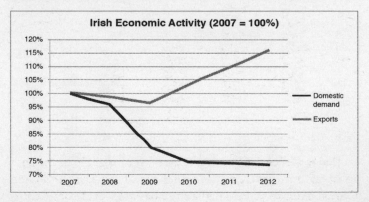

Source: *Author's calculations based on* CSO *data.*

The collapse of domestic demand has been fatal for many businesses in the hospitality and retail sectors. Family firms that survived famine, rebellion and world wars have not survived this crisis. We need to consider hard the question: is their failure due to them suddenly going soft or is it due to economic conditions that are especially toxic? With similar economic disasters afflicting Greece, Spain and Portugal, is it not more likely that these failures are largely down to Ireland's membership of the euro?

THE COLLAPSE IN PUBLIC FINANCES

Collapsing property prices, wealth and domestic demand had a severe knock-on effect on government tax revenues. Annual tax revenues fell from over €47 billion in 2007 to less than €32 billion in 2010 (see Figure 3.8). This represented a drop of one third. The situation would have been even worse had Budget 2009 and the 2009 Supplementary Budget not pursued additional revenues of €5.6 billion (through the health levy, the income levy and changes to PRSI).

Figure 3.8: There Was a Sharp Drop in Government Tax Revenues

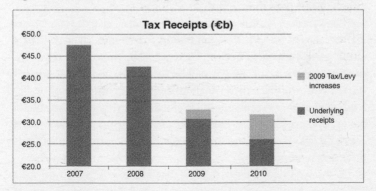

Source: *Author's calculations based on Department of Finance data.*

Had it not been for the increased taxes brought in by the 2009 measures, 2010 tax revenues would have been just €26 billion. That would have represented a drop of 45 per cent compared to 2007 receipts.

THE BANK CRASH

The collapse in the Irish economy, more specifically the collapse in property values, put immense pressure on Irish banks. Having lent so much to finance property development, the banks were exposed to the huge risk of loan losses if those developments faltered. And those losses were so large as to threaten the banks' solvency. In other words, the value of the banks' assets might have fallen below the value of their liabilities, leaving them with negative equity.

But Irish banks were also exposed to another serious problem that was less commonly understood. They were overly reliant on funding sources that could easily dry up. Normally banks aim to finance the vast bulk of their financial liabilities from customer deposits. This is because deposits represent a stable source of finance which doesn't tend to bolt and run even in the face of very bad news. The funding problem that Irish banks faced in the boom years, however, was that their customer deposits weren't growing nearly as fast as their loan books. Irish banks needed another source of funding. So they turned to the financial markets to borrow money. With the extra monies borrowed from financial markets, they were in a position to sustain an annual loan growth rate of 25 per cent and higher.

The problem with borrowing money from financial markets is that it can dry up quickly. One reason is that a lot of this money is lent on a short-term basis – for maybe 90 days or 360 days – in the expectation that the loan will be renewed when it falls due for repayment. Another reason is that the individuals controlling the lending of money are largely professionals working in international banks, who are much more skilled in evaluating bank finances than regular depositors and much more flexible in moving money from one bank to another.

In the summer of 2007, a bank that was overly reliant on such short-term funding sources ran into serious difficulties. This was Northern Rock in Britain. As Northern Rock's loan growth had fast outpaced its deposit growth, it had to fund itself increasingly with money market (or non-deposit) funding raised in financial markets. Northern Rock achieved notoriety for becoming the first British bank in 150 years to suffer a bank run after it needed to

approach the Bank of England for a loan facility to replace money
market funding that had dried up.

Irish banks had seen a steady and inexorable rise in their non-
deposit funding in the years running up to 2008. This can be seen
in Figure 3.9, which charts the relationship between the loans and
deposits of the Irish banks. As loans grew faster than deposits, the
banks became increasingly reliant on financial market funding to
make up the gap.

Figure 3.9: *Loan/Deposit Ratio of Main Irish Banks*

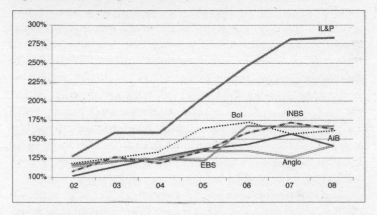

Source: Nyberg Report, p. 40.

By the autumn of 2008, loan growth far outpaced deposit
growth and Irish banks were vulnerable to the same sort of financial
avalanche that had forced the British government to rescue
Northern Rock. Irish Life & Permanent (IL&P) was particularly
vulnerable. Then, on 15 September 2008, Lehman Brothers in the
US went bust and triggered a financial avalanche.

It was known that Lehman was facing problems, but it was
believed that because of its systemic importance as a bank the US
authorities would not let it go bust for fear of the financial contagion
that might be unleashed: if Lehman went bust, there was a good
chance that interbank lending markets would dry up. This was what
happened in the autumn of 2008 and subsequently.

Before Lehman's failure, investors and lenders had believed there was an implicit government guarantee for such banks. On 15 September 2008 that belief was exposed as wrong. A contagion of fear threatened to push the global economy into a depression. Across the globe, banks suddenly became much more careful in their lending to other banks. Irish banks, especially IL&P, fell victim to this reappraisal. It is notable that, as the liquidity crisis in Irish banking unfolded, official concern centred on IL&P.[17] Thus, a 20 September report by Morgan Stanley focussed exclusively on IL&P. And the publicly released version of a 29 September memo by Merrill Lynch, setting out the options for the Irish government, had critical parts redacted (blacked out) in the case of one financial institution only: IL&P.

THE BANK GUARANTEE
By the evening of 29 September the funding situation of the Irish banking system had reached crisis point. Funding for Irish banks had dried up. A bank crash loomed. The official version of the story is that the chairmen of the two largest banks, AIB and Bank of Ireland, called for a meeting with the Taoiseach and Minister for Finance to discuss the deteriorating financing situation at the Irish banks. The unofficial version of the story has them meeting to discuss what to do about Anglo Irish Bank. In reality, the deteriorating situation at IL&P also compelled the Irish government to take action. Also present at this all-night meeting were the great and the good of Irish financial regulation, including the Governor of the Central Bank John Hurley and the Financial Regulator Pat Neary. With funding drying up, the options facing the government were frighteningly limited.

Option 1 – Do Nothing
Had nothing been done, Anglo and IL&P would have soon run out of funding from financial markets and a Northern Rock-like bank run by retail depositors would have been unleashed. With the Irish authorities sitting on the sidelines, that bank run could have soon enveloped all Irish banks and brought the entire sector to a rapid standstill.

Option 2 – Provide Emergency Loans but No Guarantee

Emergency loans might have staved off immediate problems with a limited commitment from the authorities. However, it is likely that this commitment would have been tested by the markets as other funding lines to Irish banks needed to be replaced. Rather than be caught in a drip-feed of ever greater commitment to the Irish banking sector, the authorities probably decided that it was preferable to get ahead of the markets and offer the banks a full guarantee.

Option 3 – Stand Back and Wait for the European Cavalry to Arrive

This was a real option open to the authorities. But we see in retrospect that the European authorities have been slow to move when asked to set a new policy precedent. For example, the EU delayed a long time before recognising, in April 2010, that it needed to bail out Greece. The EU had insisted that governments should bail out banks, instead of forcing bank depositors or senior bond investors to suffer losses; however, it recognised the need for the latter in the case of Cyprus in March 2013. So, had Ireland decided to wait for the EU cavalry to arrive, it would have risked a major problem. While Ireland was waiting for an answer from Frankfurt/ Brussels/Berlin, money and confidence would have been seeping out of the Irish banking system and the crisis would have got dramatically worse.

This option would have amounted to playing chicken against Europe's financial authorities, with the Irish economy as the stake.

Option 4 – Nationalise Anglo

The advantage of this option was that the government would have discovered the true state of Anglo's finances earlier and the scope for Anglo's management to engage in any future wrongdoing would have been limited. But these advantages were questionable. Five months later, in February 2009, accountants PWC gave the all-clear on Anglo's solvency, having had the opportunity to carefully examine the bank's loan book.[18]

And there would have been a significant disadvantage to nationalisation. The government was advised in September 2008 by its financial advisors Merrill Lynch that Anglo was solvent. Merrill Lynch's advice was that 'liquidity concerns aside, all of the Irish banks are profitable and well-capitalized.'[19] If Anglo was solvent, on what legal basis would the government have then nationalised it?

Option 5 – Offer a Guarantee Limited to New Deposits

While agreeing that 'an extensive guarantee needed to be put in place, since all participants (rightly) felt that they faced the likely collapse of the Irish banking system within days in the absence of decisive immediate action', Professor Patrick Honohan questioned the extent of the guarantee.

> Nevertheless, the extent of the cover provided (including to outstanding long-term bonds) can – even without the benefit of hindsight – be criticised inasmuch as it complicated and narrowed the eventual resolution options for the failing institutions and increased the State's potential share of the losses.[20]

Honohan noted, however, that these outstanding long-term bonds accounted for only a small amount of the total guarantee.

Conclusion

While there has been much political controversy over the bank guarantee, by late September 2008 the options available to the Irish government were very limited and unattractive. There is no doubt that there was a failure to understand what was going on. The authorities persisted in believing that Ireland's banks were suffering from a funding/liquidity problem rather than a solvency/negative equity problem. But they were bolstered in this position by their internal advisors the Central Bank and the Financial Regulator, and by their external advisors Merrill Lynch. And this mistaken analysis of the problem was reinforced five months later by PWC. So just how were those crafting Irish government policy in this area – namely, Taoiseach Brian Cowen and Minister for Finance Brian Lenihan – supposed to know then what later became clear to everyone? Just how could Cowen, a country solicitor, and

Lenihan, a city barrister, have known in September 2008 that the Irish banking system was fundamentally insolvent?

INVESTIGATIONS INTO A DEBACLE

As the scale of Ireland's financial and economic crisis became clear, there was a growing realisation at the heart of the Establishment that a public explanation of how things had come to this point would be required. There was also a worry that, if the Establishment didn't offer its own explanations, the public might draw the 'wrong' conclusions as to what had happened. So the Department of Finance set about initiating not one but four half-inquiries, which took place in private and examined various aspects of what had gone wrong. The terms of reference of these inquiries prevented names being named or individual guilt being attributed. And the multiplicity of inquiries had the effect of dampening the impact of any one inquiry. From an official news management perspective, this was like a forest manager inducing four controlled fires to avoid the risk of an uncontrolled conflagration, in this case one big public inquiry with the power to pass adverse conclusions on individuals. In terms of a public inquiry, the public was to be given several Chicken McNuggets rather than something resembling a T-bone steak.

Honohan Report

Professor Patrick Honohan came to public prominence during the financial and economic crisis as Ireland's international expert in banking crises. He had worked for the IMF, the World Bank, the ESRI and as a professor at Trinity College Dublin (TCD) before being appointed Governor of the Irish Central Bank in September 2009. He had earlier worked as economic advisor to Taoiseach Garret FitzGerald in the 1980s.

The Honohan Report was completed by him in May 2010. The report sought to answer two questions: first, why was the danger from the emerging imbalances in the financial system that led to the crisis not identified more clearly and earlier, and headed off through decisive measures? Second, when the crisis began to break, were the best containment measures adopted?

Perhaps the finding of the report that attracted the most public attention was that Ireland's crisis was three quarters home-grown. This contrasted with something that Professor Honohan had written just one year earlier. In a May 2009 article 'What Went Wrong in Ireland?' he had concluded with the summary:

> *Among the triggers for the property bubble was the sharp fall in interest rates following euro membership: within the euro zone also the disciplines of the market which had traditionally served as warning signs of excess were muted. Lacking these prompts, Irish policymakers neglected the basics of public finance, wage policy and bank regulation.*[21]

A few months later, in September 2009, Honohan became a member of the Governing Council of the ECB, a position in which he had to uphold European Monetary Union. In his May 2010 report he overlooked EMU when allocating blame. Instead, he concluded that our financial crisis was largely 'home-made'.

The intellectual justification for this conclusion was a graph on page 32 of his report. Honohan projected what economic growth would have been between 2007 and 2010 had Ireland enjoyed the same rate of growth as the eurozone. Comparing that to the growth which actually transpired, he then concluded that 'about three quarters of this [Ireland's loss in economic output] can be attributed to local factors.'[22] This was analysis by crayon. It wholly ignored the varying effects of monetary, fiscal and regulatory policy in the different eurozone member states. It ignored the damaging effects which large debt loads exert on economic growth. It ignored similar debt crises that erupted across the periphery of the eurozone, where interest rates had been too low for national circumstances for a decade. The finding that Ireland's crisis was 'three quarters home-made' was therefore of little merit.

Honohan did correctly conclude that 'In an important sense, major responsibility lies with the directors and senior managements of the banks that got into trouble.' But was it not rather odd that Honohan failed to criticise the board of the Central Bank? Was the board not as responsible for the well-documented failures of the Central Bank and the Financial Regulator as commercial bank boards were for the well-documented failures at those banks?

Regling Report

The Regling Report was published in June 2010. It was, in fact, the work of Klaus Regling and Max Watson. Regling is a former German government official who had been the European Commission's Director-General for Economic and Financial Affairs (DG ECFIN). He has since been appointed head of the European Stability Fund (ESF). Watson is a British academic and former IMF official. The very first line of the report's executive summary set out its key conclusion: Ireland's problems were largely home-made.

> *Ireland's banking crisis bears the clear imprint of global influences, yet it was in crucial ways 'home-made'.*[23]

In an ironic turn, Regling identified fiscal policy as the first 'home-made' factor: 'Fiscal policy heightened the vulnerability of the economy.'[24] For, just over two years earlier, in March 2008, the DG ECFIN, which he then headed up, had concluded that Ireland's fiscal policy was in order right at the very height of the bubble:

> *Despite the weakening in the budgetary position in 2007, the medium-term objective, which is a balanced position in structural terms, was reached by a large margin.*[25]

In order to bolster the argument that loose fiscal policy had contributed to the crisis, the report referenced EU Commission warnings from 2001. Facing a looming general election, those warnings had been brusquely rebuffed by then Minister for Finance Charlie McCreevy. Having secured re-election and re-appointment in 2002, McCreevy promptly slammed on the spending brakes. Ironically, it was partly the political unpopularity which accompanied this fiscal rigour that led to McCreevy's 2004 political banishment when he was appointed European Commissioner. This episode, and its implications for politicians who wanted to put the public finances on the right track, went unmentioned in the Regling Report.

The report found space to criticise the IMF, stating, 'The IMF's Financial System Stability Assessment of 2006 is not a document that warns strongly of mounting risks.'[26] But, again, there was no mention of the EU's complacent conclusion, which was given much later, in March 2008. In fairness, the report did admit that euro membership had, at the very least, contributed to Ireland's problems:

> Was it a coincidence that Ireland's economic fundamentals began to deteriorate when Ireland joined the euro area? Certain aspects of EMU membership certainly reinforced vulnerabilities in the economy. Short-term interest rates fell by two thirds from the early- and mid-90s to the period 2002–07. Long-term interest rates halved. Real interest rates were negative from 1999 to 2005 after having been strongly positive earlier. This contributed to the credit boom, the strong increase in household debt, the property bubble and the general overheating of the economy.[27]

But the report countered this point by arguing that being a member of a large monetary union had helped Ireland to better survive the global financial crisis.

Wright Report
Rob Wright reported in December 2010 'to examine the Department of Finance's performance over the last ten years and advise how the Department might adapt to meet the challenges of the future.'[28] Wright complained that 'With very few exceptions, however, the quantum of spending and tax relief outlined in December Budgets was very substantially above that advocated by the Department and Minister in June.'[29] He reached this conclusion in the face of two factors which might explain the phenomenon he bemoaned. First, there is always an element of negotiation gamesmanship in the budgetary process. Thus initial positions may be deliberately exaggerated in an attempt to improve the eventual outcome of those negotiations. Second,

between 1997 and 2007, Irish government tax revenues were rising at an annual rate of 10 per cent. It would therefore be surprising if spending totals planned in December weren't significantly higher than those initially planned in June. Despite having been a deputy finance minister in his native Canada, neither of these points appears to have occurred to Wright.

The report's conclusion, that 'advice prepared by the Department for Cabinet did provide clear warnings on the risks of pro-cyclical fiscal action,'[30] was dramatically strengthened in media reports, following official briefings. Thus RTÉ reported: 'An independent review of the performance of the Department of Finance over the past decade has found that the Department did warn the Government about the dangers of the economic policy it was following, but that its advice was overruled by the Cabinet.'[31] But that RTÉ report was simply not true. There had been no Department of Finance warning that was overruled by the Cabinet. Yet senior officials sought to portray things otherwise. The absence, in the entirety of the report, of a single direct quote of any such warning is notable.

Official media briefings should not have been allowed to obscure the rather obvious central conclusion that Wright reached: 'The Department of Finance should have done more to avoid this outcome.'[32]

Nyberg Report

The Nyberg Report was produced in March 2011 by a Finnish academic who had previously occupied senior roles in his country's finance ministry and Central Bank. But, while Nyberg may have been an outsider in terms of nationality, he was an insider in institutional terms. And his terms of reference precluded an examination of any role played in Ireland's crisis by its membership of the European common currency area. Nyberg was formally charged with providing 'answers on why a number of institutions, both private and public, acted in an imprudent or ineffective manner, thereby contributing to the occurrence of the Irish banking crisis.'[33] Despite these shortcomings, Nyberg did good work and reached a number of important conclusions. He

did point out the importance of cheap European credit, although
he downplayed this factor:

> *Entry into the euro area markedly reduced Irish interest rates.*
> *Banks had increased access to market funding, where cheap and*
> *abundant credit was already available owing to monetary policies*
> *in major countries as well as the increasing use of securitisation.*
> *... Though eventually unsustainable financial risks were made*
> *attractive by outside factors, there simply was nobody abroad*
> *forcing Irish authorities, banks or investors to accept such risks.*[34]

Nyberg was sharply critical of the roles played by the Central
Bank (CB) and Financial Regulator (FR):

> *The CB was not powerless; it had the right to direct the activities*
> *of the FR and it could advise the Government. There are, however,*
> *no records of such direction or advice or even efforts at such.*
> *   The CB had a pivotal position, itself contributing to overall*
> *financial stability and being able to direct the FR. In the view*
> *of the Commission, macroeconomic developments were already*
> *exhibiting signs in 2005–2006 that reasonably should have caused*
> *concerns in the CB. However during the Period in question, it did*
> *not take forceful measures but largely confined itself to providing*
> *reminders of existing risks.... There may have been a state of*
> *denial in the CB; warnings of stability risks appear to have been*
> *sidestepped internally or, when made public especially in the*
> *Financial Stability Reports, toned down in the policy conclusions.*
> *Trust in a soft landing was consistent and, though not very well*
> *founded, continued up until and including the crisis management*
> *phase of the Period.*[35]

But while Nyberg did point to individual symptoms, he failed
to connect them towards a wholly plausible explanation of what
had happened. Was it plausible to blame individual institutions in
Ireland for corporate failure, 'herding' and 'groupthink' without
addressing the wholly subversive effect of a decade of ultra-cheap
eurozone credit? And was it plausible to largely blame the crisis

on national failings when similar crises with a similar background
were simultaneously erupting all across the eurozone periphery?
The failure of Nyberg to refer to that Central Bank warning of April
1999 was notable. It would appear that nobody informed him of it.

Could it be that the Central Bank preferred to be condemned
for negligence, in not foreseeing what might go wrong, than for
moral cowardice, in warning of what might go wrong but later
ceasing to make such warnings as they appeared misplaced?
The Central Bank's stance – of issuing a warning in 1999 and
subsequently issuing reassuring commentary as late as 2007 –
contrasted with the stance of the former Central Bank economist
David McWilliams. Like the Irish Central Bank, he warned in the
late 1990s of the dangers of overheating in Irish property prices as a
result of cheap credit. Unlike the Irish Central Bank, he repeatedly
maintained his position that there was a bubble even though he
had to wait many years for vindication. People may argue that his
warning was premature. But McWilliams warned of the bubble
when there was still time to do something about it. By 2006 and
2007, when some prominent economists joined him in issuing
warnings, most of the financial damage had already been done and
it was then too late for Ireland to avoid a severe crash.

For his foresight and steadfastness, McWilliams has found few
friends in the Establishment. An exasperated Garret FitzGerald no
doubt had McWilliams in mind when he referred dismissively to
'celebrity economists'. But the fact is that McWilliams's accurate
diagnosis of a bubble and explanation of its reasons (ultra-low
eurozone interest rates) robs the Establishment economists who
got it wrong of the alibi that 'nobody could have foreseen this'.
McWilliams foresaw it but they didn't. His persistent prescience
robs them of an excuse for their consistent complacency.

Conclusion

The official reports into Ireland's economic and financial disaster
had a number of points in common. While they admitted that
cheap eurozone interest rates contributed to the crisis, they denied
the central role which euro membership had played. Thus, Ireland's
crisis was considered on its own rather than in the context of

similar crises developing simultaneously in Greece, Spain, Portugal, Cyprus, etc. We were to believe that this problem was all, or nearly all, of our own making rather than just one element of a continent-wide crisis. The feckless Paddies were to blame rather than pie-in-the-sky Europeans of questionable competence playing Lego with currency systems, the workings of which they didn't understand.

Truly hard questions were not asked of the key institutions that had grievously failed Ireland. For example, it was alleged that the Department of Finance had warned the government about the dangers of its economic policy and that these warnings had been overruled. But, rather implausibly, no single example of such a warning was produced to support this assertion. Similarly, Honohan's justified criticism of the boards of commercial banks was unaccompanied by any criticism of the board of the Central Bank, which was surely guilty of a much greater failure. After all, it was aware of warnings dating back to 1999 and it was responsible for the stability of the entire financial system. Another aspect that these reports had in common was that, while the institutions that had failed Ireland were named, the individuals responsible were not.

These reports must be seen as a coordinated – and largely successful – exercise in the formation and conditioning of public opinion by Ireland's government Establishment. We Irish were responsible for becoming debt junkies – the EU enablers who happily supplied us with debt bore little or no responsibility. The great institutions of the State had made some serious mistakes, but these were now identified and the situation rectified so that there would be no recurrence.

The failure by these reports to name names inevitably resulted in public debate focussing on known and elected public servants – such as former Taoisigh Bertie Ahern and Brian Cowen – rather than on little-known, unelected public officials in the Department of Finance, Central Bank and Financial Regulator. It may be argued that, in political terms, this was fair. As US President Harry Truman said, 'The buck stops here,' and Ireland's political leadership must take responsibility for regulatory failure. But, in law, the buck for central banking and regulation does not stop with Ireland's Minister for Finance or head of government. As we have already seen, Treaty law had made central bankers institutionally independent across the EU. Remarkably, in over 400 pages of combined reportage, Honohan, Regling and Nyberg failed to make even a single explicit reference to this critical legal and institutional point.

The intellectual failures of these reports to accurately assess the situation in hindsight contrast sharply with the intellectual accuracy shown before the event by British Treasury official Derek Mitchell. He wrote a secret note for his political masters in 1972 on the implications of a possible monetary union in Europe. That note warned against European Monetary Union (EMU):

> *Full EMU would deprive member countries of many of the policy instruments needed to influence their economic performances and (particularly in the case of the exchange rate) to rectify imbalances between them. . . . In an EMU, equilibrium could only then be restored by inflation in the 'high performance' countries and stagnation in the 'low performance' countries, unless central provision is made for the imbalances to be offset by massive and speedy resource transfers.*[36]

While the remedy outlined by Mitchell to correct internal imbalances (inflation in the 'high performance' countries and stagnation in the 'low performance' ones) may be intellectually correct, it is politically impossible as long as 'high performance' Germany refuses to tolerate higher inflation. And that is exactly the case. Former German Chancellor Gerhard Schröder has been explicit in excluding the possibility, saying, 'Now that Germany has gone through a difficult time, lowered its costs and has recovered competitiveness, the other countries have to do the same. There is no way that Germany is going to produce significantly more inflation to help out the others.'[37]

Meanwhile, trapped in a deflationary spiral and clinging to an incorrect analysis of what happened, Official Ireland grasps Plan A even more tightly.

04 PLAN A

Power always thinks it has a great soul and vast views beyond the comprehension of the weak; and that it is doing God's service when it is violating all his laws.

John Quincy Adams,
sixth President of the US

PATRICK HONOHAN RIDES TO THE RESCUE

Patrick Honohan is widely respected by the Irish public. He came to his job as Central Bank Governor as a fresh wind of change. Instead of a superannuated dusty insider from the Department of Finance, we got a respected TCD economics professor and academic expert in banking crises, with many years' experience at the World Bank where he was Senior Financial Sector Advisor. But, for an expert in banking crises and financial sector policy, Honohan showed disappointingly little evidence that he anticipated Ireland's looming banking sector collapse.

As late as June 2008, Honohan gave a presentation to an EU Commission workshop entitled 'Another Lap for the Irish Hare?' While the paper did identify 'some financial vulnerability', it failed to contemplate the possibility that Ireland's banks faced impending disaster. Instead, Honohan's paper concluded that 'scale growth could resume' for the Irish economy.[1] More than five years later, Ireland still waits for a return to meaningful economic growth and our banks remain in intensive care. Reviewing Honohan's June 2008 presentation, it is hard to avoid the conclusions that Ireland's leading expert on financial sector policy misread what was happening in the Irish economy at the time, and that he failed to anticipate the tsunami about to hit our banks.

Despite this failure, Honohan was an obvious candidate when the Irish economic Establishment was looking for a new Governor of the Central Bank. His credentials were impeccable. He helped his chances of becoming Governor of the Central Bank when he suggested that the banks should share the burden of any losses that might be made by the National Asset Management Agency (NAMA). That argument appealed to Fianna Fáil and Green Party ministers, who, back in 2009, were exasperated at the cost of rescuing Ireland's banking system. The idea assumed that the Irish banking system had net worth that could be used to reduce the State's NAMA losses. However, as it later emerged that Ireland's banking system was hopelessly insolvent, it is hard to avoid the conclusion that Honohan had, once again, misread the financial state of Ireland's banks.

As a senior World Bank official, Honohan co-wrote a paper in 2000 entitled 'Controlling the Fiscal Costs of Banking Crises'. The author found that:

> [u]nlimited deposit guarantees, open-ended liquidity support, repeated recapitalization, debtor bail-outs, and regulatory forbearance add significantly and sizeably to costs.[2]

All of the measures which Honohan concluded 'add greatly to the fiscal cost of banking crises' are now being practised in Ireland, with policies over which he exerts determinative influence. One could argue that the policies were set in place before his appointment and that, with the ECB breathing down his neck, Honohan has limited room for manoeuvre. But it is nonetheless striking that he practises today the very opposite of what he preached yesterday.

The personnel and corporate governance arrangements in Honohan's Central Bank are also striking. In obvious breach of the most elementary rule of good corporate governance, Honohan occupies both the chairman and chief executive positions at Ireland's Central Bank. And, while it was generally assumed that those who were in key positions at the commercial banks when the crash hit would vacate their positions, the opposite seems to apply at the Central Bank.

When Honohan reported on the origins of Ireland's financial
and economic crisis in May 2010, public attention centred on one
conclusion: that our crisis was largely 'home-made'. He also stated
that, of Ireland's loss in economic output, 'about three quarters
of this can be attributed to local factors.'[3] The notion that the
roots of the crisis could have been in our membership of the euro
was simply side-stepped and ignored. Instead, we Irish were to
blame. That message very much suited Honohan's new colleagues
and masters in Frankfurt. For, by the autumn of 2010, they were
unhappy with Ireland once more. Over the summer of 2010, a
steady outflow of bank deposits required emergency funding from
the ECB to avoid our banks closing down. By that autumn, over
one third of the Irish banking system's total funding (an amount
in excess of €150 billion) was coming from emergency Central
Bank deposits.

The ECB decided that enough was enough and lobbied to
put Ireland into the economic care of the Troika (EU, ECB and
IMF). The government, and especially Minister for Finance Brian
Lenihan, fought back by arguing that the State had plenty of funding
arranged. But would our banks have been able to fund themselves
if the ECB had pulled the plug? The answer to that question was
clearly no. Blackmailed by this threat, the Irish government was
pushed into a corner but continued to fight on. And then, on the
morning of 18 November 2010, Governor Honohan stated in an
RTÉ interview that IMF officials were in town to negotiate 'a very
substantial loan' for Ireland. Three days later the government
capitulated and formally applied to the Troika for that loan. As
Brian Lenihan said, 'I had fought for two and a half years to avoid
this conclusion. I believed I had fought the good fight and taken
every measure possible to delay such an eventuality. And now hell
was at the gates.'

Part of the Troika agreement required a restructuring, or
significant downsizing, of Ireland's banks. As a result, in March
2011, the Irish government agreed to pump €24 billion of our
money into Ireland's ailing banks. At that time, Honohan asserted
that that figure was only appropriate in an 'adverse and unlikely'
situation. Yet, today, the Irish banking system is readying itself

for fresh stress tests to see if it needs yet more of our money. The 'adverse and unlikely' scenario of yesteryear has become today's baseline scenario.

In October 2011, at a major government-organised conference held at Farmleigh, former US President Bill Clinton identified mortgage debt as Ireland's biggest problem. More than two years have passed since those comments and more than five years have passed since the start of Ireland's economic crisis. Yet the evidence of bank chief executives at Oireachtas hearings in September 2013 indicated that hardly any tangible progress had been made in fixing the critical problem of mortgage arrears. The official body responsible for implementing public policy in this area is the Central Bank, under Governor Patrick Honohan.

THE KEY ELEMENTS OF PLAN A

The authorities' Plan A to solve Ireland's economic calamity comprised several elements, the implementation of which began long before Honohan was appointed to head up the Irish Central Bank.

Element 1: Rescue the Banks with Capital Infusions from the Taxpayer

It was the threat that Ireland's banks would be unable to finance themselves that pushed the Irish government into issuing the September 2008 bank guarantee. Having just guaranteed €440 billion of bank debt, Official Ireland remained remarkably complacent. But the pattern of events,[4] and its belated reaction to them, would expose the Fianna Fáil–Green Party government to eventual electoral annihilation.

An initial belief that the government could make money from charging for a liquidity guarantee that would never be used was gradually replaced by the recognition of the hard reality: Ireland's banks had lost mountains of money by making questionable loans and Ireland's national solvency was now threatened by the insolvency of the country's commercial banks. And only infusions of fresh equity by Irish taxpayers would prevent the appalling vista of Ireland's banks shutting down in disarray and unleashing

financial chaos across the land. That recognition was slow in
coming, as a dismal catalogue of contemporaneous comments and
events makes clear:

• September 2008 – Minister for Finance Brian Lenihan asserted,
  'We are not in the business here of bailing out banks.'
• October 2008 – Lenihan said that the bank guarantee was 'the
  cheapest bailout in the world so far'.
• December 2008 – the government announced it would inject
  up to €7.5 billion into the State's three main banks, AIB, Bank
  of Ireland and Anglo Irish Bank. 'The investment reflects our
  assessment of what is required to meet the challenges they face,'
  said Brian Lenihan.
• January 2009 – the Government didn't proceed with its planned
  €1.5 billion injection into Anglo Irish Bank and nationalised it
  instead.
• February 2009 – the recapitalisation of AIB and Bank of Ireland
  went ahead, but the figure had increased to €3.5 billion for each
  bank.
• April 2009 – on the day of the Emergency or Supplementary
  Budget, the Government admitted that AIB would need
  another €1.5 billion, which the bank said it would raise
  itself. The Government announced that it was setting up the
  National Asset Management Agency (NAMA). This state 'bad
  bank' would buy up stressed loans from commercial banks.
  This model had been successfully applied elsewhere. The
  supposed advantages of it were that, first, it would free banks
  from managing problem loans to allow them to concentrate on
  good loans and on new lending and, second, while commercial
  banks might not wish to admit the full scale of their problems,
  a switch to state ownership would force rapid discovery of the
  true state of affairs.
• May 2009 – Lenihan told the Dáil that Anglo Irish Bank would
  need more capital. Losses at the bank were 'somewhat beyond
  expectation', the Minister said. At the end of the month, the
  government confirmed it would inject up to €4 billion into

Anglo, on top of the €7 billion already invested in AIB and Bank of Ireland.

- March 2010 – as the Government tried to quantify the 'black holes' at the banks, it emerged that AIB would require €7.4 billion and Bank of Ireland €2.7 billion. Anglo Irish Bank was said to need €8.3 billion on top of the €4 billion already earmarked. Building societies Irish Nationwide and EBS required €2.7 billion and €875 million respectively, and both would end up in effective state control. Lenihan said the recapitalisation plan for the banks would draw a line under the financial crisis 'once and for all'.

- March 2010 – Lenihan said Anglo might require an additional €10 billion of taxpayers' money to meet future losses on NAMA loans. This would be on top of the monies already invested. Lenihan confessed, 'At every hand's turn, our worst fears have been surpassed.'

- April 2010 – Alan Dukes, the chairman designate of Anglo Irish Bank, said he could not rule out the need for further state investment beyond the €22.3 billion bailout already set aside for the bank. 'I'd love to say that would be the end of it, but I can't with any confidence say that,' he said.

- August 2010 – Central Bank Governor Patrick Honohan put the net cost to the Government of recapitalising Anglo Irish Bank at 'about €22–25 billion' and said that the cost of propping up Irish Nationwide Building Society could rise from €2.7 billion to €3.2 billion.

- September 2010 – the Central Bank said Anglo would need €29.3 billion in capital, while an additional €5 billion might be required 'under a severe hypothetical stress scenario'. Irish Nationwide Building Society was said to need a further €2.7 billion, bringing its total to €5.4 billion. The Central Bank also revealed that AIB needed to raise another €3 billion, which the State would underwrite. Lenihan said the level of state support to the banking system 'remains manageable' and that the figures represented the 'rock bottom' of the financial crisis.[5]

Public attention focussed, understandably, on the gigantic loan losses of the Irish banks and on the alarming amounts of fresh equity which the banks then needed from taxpayers in order to stay open. But there was another, even more acute, problem facing Ireland's financial institutions. Like nearly every business, banks don't go out of business when they run out of equity; they go out of business when they run out of cash. And behind the scenes Ireland's banks were running out of cash as depositors pulled their money out.

Ireland's banks faced a bank run. But it was a modern bank run. It wasn't average depositors and small savers who were pulling out their deposits; it was professional depositors at other banks, insurance companies and financial institutions. And they didn't queue up in the street waiting to pull out their money; they withdrew their money electronically. So even though Ireland's banks faced a fully-fledged bank run, there was little public recognition of this alarming reality. But a look at the deposit picture at Ireland's six main banks[6] confirms this alarming reality (see Figure 4.1).

Figure 4.1: Irish Banks Were Hit by a Low-Level Bank Run

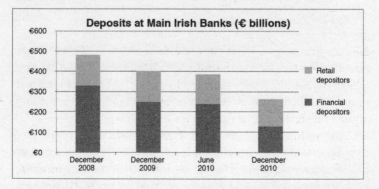

Source: *Central Bank (2013)*, The Financial Measures Programme Report, *March, available from:* http://www.centralbank.ie, *accessed January 2014, chart 5, p. 40.*

The government's September 2008 bank guarantee was meant to stabilise the funding and deposit situation at Ireland's banks. But between December 2008 and December 2010, the Irish banking system endured deposit outflows totalling €222 billion.

Retail depositors withdrew a relatively modest €18 billion, while professional depositors based in capital markets, companies and banks pulled out an astonishing €204 billion. So in the two years following December 2008, deposit funding at Irish banks dropped by nearly half. Only access to emergency Central Bank funding stood between Ireland's banks and the abyss. And, in fairness to the ECB and the Irish Central Bank, that everyday funding was forthcoming. The problem was that alarmingly large deposit outflows required alarmingly large Central Bank emergency liquidity support (see Table 4.1).

Table 4.1: Emergency Liquidity Support for Irish Banks

	€ billions
August 2010	€96
September 2010	€119
October 2010	€131

Source: Central Bank (2013), Financial Statements, November, available from: http://www. centralbank.ie, accessed January 2014, Table A.2.

Public and political attention in Ireland was focussed on the gap between government spending and government revenue – in 2010 this was running at about €20 billion each year. But the ECB's attention was focussed on the outflow of funds from Ireland's banks, which, by autumn 2010, was running at nearly €20 billion each month. By October that year, emergency funding was providing around one third of total funding for the Irish banking system.

The authorities at the ECB became increasingly alarmed that they would be the eventual losers in a fast-moving game of financial pass-the-parcel. So, in the five weeks that began on 15 October 2010, the President of the ECB Jean-Claude Trichet sent three letters to Ireland's Minister for Finance Brian Lenihan. He pointed out the extent of ECB support for the Irish banking system. But he warned that this exposure was too great and could even pose a threat to the stability of the entire European banking system. The bottom line was that continued support for Ireland's banks would depend on the Irish government applying for a bailout from the Troika. Like parents who had guaranteed their child's loan and were now getting nasty calls from the bank, the Irish government was getting nasty calls over the borrowings of the Irish commercial banking system. Its negotiations with the Troika were based on the fiction that the Irish government had requested the Troika to come to its aid. Thus, the December 2010 documents which formed the basis of the agreement with the Troika took the form of a letter from the Irish authorities setting out their intentions.[7] That letter was co-signed by Minister for Finance Brian Lenihan and Central Bank Governor Patrick Honohan.

Their letter – which stretched to 44 pages when appendices were included – featured some words of cardinal importance: 'a fundamental downsizing and reorganisation of our banking system is essential.' In the years that followed, the Irish public was told that its banks were open for business as usual. Television and other media advertisements underlined that message. But the banks were not open for business as usual. They were undergoing 'a fundamental downsizing'. A few months later, in March 2011, the Central Bank published its detailed plan for the Irish banking sector.

The Financial Measures Programme Report[8] aimed to address the two big problems left facing the Irish banking sector due to the huge property loan losses, both current and future. First, the State would have to invest substantial amounts of fresh equity capital in order to make good the losses foreseen by the stress tests, an outline of which accompanied the report. Second, the banking sector would have to reduce its overall lending in order to reduce its dependence on deposits from the fickle financial sector. A reduction of over €70 billion in the combined lending of AIB, Bank of Ireland, EBS and Irish Life & Permanent was envisaged over the three years (2011–13) encompassed by the plan (see Table 4.2).

Table 4.2: Net Lending (€ billions)

Bank	December 2010	December 2013	Change
AIB	€86.9	€67.5	-€19.4
BOI	€115.3	€82.7	-€32.6
EBS	€16.4	€11.5	-€4.9
ILP	€37.0	€21.3	-€15.7
Total	€255.6	€183.0	-€72.6

Source: *Central Bank (2011)*, The Financial Measures Programme Report, *March, available from: http://www.centralbank.ie, Table 6, p. 13.*

It is true that a large portion of these loan book reductions were to be achieved by reductions in lending beyond the island of Ireland. But other entities would be reducing their Irish lending as well: the loan books of Anglo Irish Bank and Irish Nationwide Building Society were being run down in their entirety; Bank of Scotland (Ireland) was exiting the market; and Ulster Bank faced severe problems of its own. The result was a credit crunch. Official statistics show that between September 2010 (just before the arrival of the Troika to Ireland) and June 2013, the total amount loaned to Irish households dropped by over 20 per cent, while the amount loaned to Irish business dropped by nearly 25 per cent.[9] When organisations representing small and medium-sized enterprises protested this fact, they were flatly told that they were wrong. But they were right.

John Eager, an experienced accountant, described the predicament facing countless Irish businesses. They were being forced to repay loans even though they were not generating any profits. In that situation, businesses had to borrow ever more from their suppliers and creditors in order to borrow less from the banks. As Eager put it, in a December 2010 article for *Accountancy Ireland*:

> *Creditor terms in particular are completely drawn out. It is not unusual to see creditor ledgers at 105 days or more. There is a mirror position – debtor days are now nationally standing at about 75 days. This is the proof that liquidity doesn't exist in Irish business. It has been drained out of working capital to pay loans that cannot be paid from profit.[10]*

But, not only did the Irish banking system have to reduce its
lending to Irish borrowers so as to reduce its own borrowings from
financial depositors, it also had to raise substantial fresh equity
capital to make up for the horrendous losses it was suffering (and
was expected to suffer) on bad loans. Based on the 2011 stress tests
carried out on Ireland's banks, Central Bank Governor Patrick
Honohan reckoned that an additional €24 billion in capital
would be needed to cover bank losses 'in an adverse and unlikely
macroeconomic scenario'. This brought the total amount pumped
into Ireland's banks by taxpayers up to €70 billion. This figure did
not include any of the €16 billion that, it was reckoned, the British
government had pumped into Ulster Bank via its parent, the Royal
Bank of Scotland.

Element 2: Rescue the Public Finances with Budgetary Austerity

If the authorities saw their first task as being the rescue of Ireland's
banking system, their second task was the restoration of order to
Ireland's public finances. The public finances had come under
huge pressure, with government spending rising as the greater
number of unemployed sought benefits, while government
revenues fell sharply as taxes from the previously booming
property sector dried up and taxes from the rest of the economy
weakened.

Annual tax revenues dropped from €44 billion in 2007 to just €32
billion in 2010. This fall of €12 billion occurred despite a combined
revenue-raising increase of over €7 billion in the budgets of 2008
and 2009. Over the same period, welfare spending grew from €15
billion to €22 billion. As a result of the collapse in tax revenues
and the strong rise in welfare spending, the government's balanced
budget position in 2007 was transformed into a catastrophic and
dangerous deficit position by 2010.

The political position that was adopted by the Fianna Fáil–
Green Party government was that this deficit must be reduced
through budgetary austerity, i.e. through a programme of tax
increases and government spending cuts. But, in truth, this
was a simple recognition of the fact that Ireland could not keep
borrowing large amounts indefinitely.

And so the government embarked on a long and difficult path to return the Irish public finances to sustainability. The scale of the expenditure cuts and tax increases was, at over 20 per cent of Irish GDP, astonishingly large (see Table 4.3). And the human cost and strain imposed by these measures was significant.

Table 4.3: Ireland's Extraordinarily Large Budgetary Adjustments

	Expenditure	*Tax*	*Other*	*Total*	% 2010 GDP
July 2008	€1,000			€1,000	0.6%
Budget 2009		€2,000		€2,000	1.3%
February 2010	€2,100			€2,100	1.4%
Supp. Budget 2009	€1,800	€3,600		€5,400	3.5%
Budget 2010	€4,100			€4,100	2.7%
Budget 2011	€4,000	€1,400	€700	€6,100	4.0%
Budget 2012	€2,200	€1,600		€3,800	2.5%
Budget 2013	€1,900	€1,600		€3,500	2.3%
	€17,100	€10,200	€700	€28,000	18.2%
Budget 2014	€2,000	€1,100		€3,100	2.0%
Budget 2015	€1,300	€700		€2,000	1.3%
Total	€20,400	€12,000	€700	€33,100	21.5%

Source: NCB Stockbrokers (2013), 'Irish Economy Monitor', Dublin, April, p. 28.

The other problem with the budgetary adjustments was that €1 gained through budgetary measures failed to translate into €1 of deficit reduction. The deficit was €13.1 billion in 2008 and €12.5 billion in 2012, despite over €20 billion of budgetary adjustments in the meantime. Ireland was like a man trying to swim back to shore in the face of a powerful riptide. Ireland was swimming bravely and expending huge energy but, facing into powerful currents, was making only very limited progress. So it was that between the end of 2007 and the end of 2012, Ireland's national debt grew from €47 billion to €193 billion. The two main drivers of the growth in the national debt were the gap of around €80 billion between regular government spending and revenue, and the circa €65 billion bailout of the banks.

Element 3: European Help for the Periphery

While the creditor states of the EU may have wanted the debtor states to fix what they saw as their own financial problems, it soon emerged that this would not be possible. The size of the peripheral states' debt loads and the economic adjustments required to restore order to their public finances were simply too much for those countries to cope with on their own. In his book *The Price of Power*, journalist Pat Leahy reports that, in 2011, some members of the incoming Fine Gael–Labour government felt that the Troika programme they had inherited from the previous government simply couldn't work. Leahy reports one person who attended early meetings of the government's Economic Management Council (EMC) as saying: 'The programme couldn't work. The numbers were just too much.'[11] And, bad and all as things were in Ireland, they were even worse in Greece and Portugal.

So the EU scrambled to help reduce the financial burdens faced by the eurozone periphery. In July 2011, European leaders agreed that they would reduce by 2 per cent the interest rate on their bailout loans to Greece, Portugal and Ireland. In earlier negotiations, the Irish government had been seeking just a 1 per cent interest rate cut. The saving eventually agreed was estimated to be worth over €10 billion over the lifetime of the loans. Later, in February 2013, Ireland won additional concessions on the notorious Anglo-Irish Bank promissory notes. The effective burden of the promissory note debt was reduced when the interest rate payable was cut and the payment term was extended. It was estimated that the effective saving from this measure was about €13 billion over the lifetime of the debt. But even after these concessions were made, the government's own Fiscal Advisory Council warned that Ireland's debt load might not be sustainable. In an April 2013 assessment, it warned that there was a 'one-in-four probability that the debt-to-GDP ratio will fail to stabilise by the end of the projection period unless further policy measures beyond those currently planned are taken'.[12] The bottom line was that Ireland's EU partners were offering us significant help, but even with that help it remained doubtful that we would be able to master our problems.

And the European authorities were just as bad as their Irish counterparts in terms of viewing their problems through rose-tinted glasses. Consider the following remarks:

- July 2010: 'The worst is over ... the IMF is underestimating the strength of the economy in Europe' – Jürgen Stark, ECB Chief Economist.

- January 2011: 'I think the Eurozone has turned the corner' – Christine Lagarde, French Minister for Finance.

- March 2012: 'The problems have not yet finished, but the worst of the crisis is over' – Herman van Rompuy, President of the European Council.

- March 2012: 'We can say that the worst is behind us, but we cannot relax our efforts' – Wolfgang Schäuble, German Minister for Finance.

- October 2012: 'The worst is over' – Francois Hollande, French President.

- November 2012: 'I'm definitely convinced that the worst has passed' – Mariano Rajoy, Spanish Prime Minister.

- December 2012: 'I believe the worst is past' – Wolfgang Schäuble, German Minister for Finance.

- January 2013: 'The crisis is not over yet, but the worst is over' – Ewald Nowotny, ECB governing council.

- January 2013: 'I think we can say that the existential threat against the euro has essentially been overcome' – José Manuel Barroso, President of the European Commission.

- January 2013: 'Firstly and most importantly, the worst is behind us, in particular the existential threat to the euro' – Herman van Rompuy, President of the European Council.

- January 2013: 'The single currency is over the worst of the crisis' – Wolfgang Schäuble, German Minister for Finance.

- January 2013: 'The worst is probably over, but what we still have to do is difficult' – Jean-Claude Juncker, President of the Eurogroup.

While the short-term aim of such remarks may have been to calm citizens and to stabilise markets, their inevitable long-term effect was to reduce public confidence that Europe's authorities actually knew what they were doing.

Element 4: European Fiscal Union?

There is one ace in the hole which Official Ireland hopes to be able to play if the elements of Plan A outlined above prove insufficient to solve Ireland's economic and financial problems: European fiscal union. Fiscal union would involve the nations of the EU giving up their national budgetary independence in order to pool sovereignty over budgetary matters at a European level. Instead of each nation state having its own budgetary kitty, there would be one big budgetary kitty in Brussels. And Ireland's public debt crisis would become a small part of Europe's debt problems. Hurrah! We could find someone else willing to take over the management of the mess we have made.

But is fiscal union likely and would it make things better or worse for Ireland? Politically, European fiscal union is not currently on the agenda. Leading political figures in countries which would end up being the largest net financial contributors have stated categorically that there will be no fiscal union. In March 2103, German Chancellor Angela Merkel stated publicly: 'I see no need in the next few years to give up more powers to the Commission in Brussels.'[13] But, in May 2010, Merkel also stated categorically that 'there is absolutely no question' of a bailout for Greece.[14] Later that same month, the EU agreed a €110 billion bailout for Greece. Merkel was reported as stating in September 2011 that no Greek debt default could happen before 2013, when the eurozone's permanent rescue fund, the European Stability Mechanism, was due to come into operation.[15] Yet, in October 2011, it was agreed that Greece would renege on €100 billion of its debts.

The evidence of the recent past is that, when financial pressures reach crisis point, top European policy-makers blink, jettison prior commitments and reach into their taxpayers' pockets to do enough to stop the eurozone problem going into complete meltdown. But do they do enough to solve the debt problems they are supposedly fixing? The answer, in the case of Greece, is a clear no. A third bailout for Greece is being contemplated.[16] It seems that European policy-makers will do enough to stop the problem becoming critical, but they won't do enough to solve the problem.

Thus, even if some form of European fiscal union became politically feasible, it is very unlikely that it would involve Ireland simply transferring its debts to the EU. Based on the Greek experience, it is much more likely that any financial help Europe gives Ireland will be the bare minimum to keep the financial show on the road.

The giddy talk in some quarters that European fiscal union could solve Ireland's debt problems also ignores a number of other important and serious problems. While some form of limited European fiscal union might eventually become politically feasible, would it be legally feasible? There have been a number of cases taken by German citizens to the German Constitutional Court (Bundesverfassungsgericht) contesting the constitutionality of the German government's agreement to various EU measures and treaties. While these cases have in the main been rejected, Germany's top judges have used them as opportunities to warn the country's politicians of legal limits concerning any further steps towards European integration.

In a June 2009 ruling, the German Constitutional Court stated that Germany's constitution 'does not grant the bodies acting on behalf of Germany powers to abandon the right to self-determination of the German people in the form of Germany's sovereignty under international law by joining a federal state'. So a federal European State is expressly ruled out under Germany's existing constitutional arrangements. The court added that the German constitution excludes the possibility 'of depleting the content of the legitimisation of state authority, and the influence on the exercise of that authority provided by the election, by transferring the responsibilities and competences of the Bundestag [Parliament] to the European level to such an extent that the principle of democracy is violated.'[17] So a change to Germany's constitution would be required before it could sign up to a Federal European Union.

Even if German political and legal obstacles can be overcome, we must face the hard question of whether Ireland would be a long-term beneficiary of European fiscal union. Ireland is one of the EU's better-off member states. Therefore, greater European financial integration will, in the long-term, lead to greater net financial contributions from Ireland. So European fiscal union may bring short-term benefits, i.e. debt sharing, but at the expense of long-term costs, i.e. a higher level of expected net contribution to Europe's coffers.

Evidence also exists that a significant sacrifice of national sovereignty would be required for Ireland to be part of a fiscal union. In June 2011, then head of the ECB Jean-Claude Trichet called for the establishment of 'a ministry of finance of the Union'. This would be a large step on the way towards eventual fiscal union. Trichet specifically called for:

> [A] ministry of finance that would exert direct responsibilities in at least three domains: first, the surveillance of both fiscal policies and competitiveness policies, as well as the direct responsibilities mentioned earlier as regards countries in a 'second stage' inside the euro area; second, all the typical responsibilities of the executive branches as regards the union's integrated financial sector, so as to accompany the full integration of financial services; and third, the representation of the union confederation in international financial institutions.[18]

The large up-front benefit which debt sharing would confer on Ireland may also come with an unpalatable up-front cost attached: a change in Ireland's corporation tax regime. For it is clear that politicians in locations as far flung as Berlin, Paris and Washington are annoyed at Irish laws facilitating the avoidance of tax by large multinationals. If the EU was to offer major help to Ireland by assuming a significant portion of our public debts, is it likely that it would ask for nothing in return?

WAYS IN WHICH THE CRISIS IS UNDERPLAYED

One of the ways in which the Irish authorities dealt with the economic crisis was to simply downplay its various symptoms and

deny its full extent. This strategy wasn't immediately obvious. But
the disturbing pattern emerges when one surveys their comments
on a broad range of problem areas.

Mortgage Arrears

On 21 June 2013, the Central Bank published mortgage arrears
data for the period ending 31 March 2013. RTÉ reported the news
on its website under the headline '12.3% of mortgages in arrears
– Central Bank'.[19] That was one way of looking at the facts. As we
already saw in Chapter 1, the Central Bank reached this figure by
ignoring a number of key elements. It could equally be argued
that 33 per cent of mortgage balances were either in arrears or had
already been restructured. The Central Bank had chosen to present
a more comforting reality.

Bank Lending

A similar situation existed in relation to bank lending. Officially,
all was well and the banks were open for business as usual. On 25
January 2009, Minister for Finance Brian Lenihan told the Dáil that
AIB and Bank of Ireland were committed to a credit package. The
measures included in this package included 'at least an additional
10 per cent capacity for lending to small to medium enterprises
in 2009'; 'an additional 30 per cent capacity for lending to first
time buyers in 2009'; and an undertaking to 'assist householders
who are in arrears on their mortgages'.[20] The political message
communicated by the Minister for Finance was backed up by
extensive media advertising, which conveyed the same message
that the banks were open for business as usual. But, in reality, the
banks were applying sharp reductions to their lending. Central
Bank statistics revealed the bitter truth. By May 2013, bank lending
to households had dropped by 31 per cent from its May 2008 peak.
The story for lending to business was even worse: this had dropped
by 52 per cent from its August 2008 peak.[21]

   In part, this was a problem of the Irish banks' own making.
But it also reflected problems in the foreign banks that had
been attracted to Ireland during the boom years but decided to
exit Ireland in the bust. The result, whatever lending initiatives

governing politicians announced, was a brutal credit crunch which
sucked credit out of the economy.

Property Prices
The residential property market felt the brunt of the credit crunch
as credit for fresh mortgages dried up. By August 2013, the total
volume of mortgage debt in Ireland had dropped by 31 per cent
from its May 2008 peak. That represented a drop of over €44 billion.
This sharp credit crunch, coupled with the extraordinarily elevated
prices Irish houses had commanded at the peak of the bubble,
triggered a fall in house prices. By June 2013, the CSO estimated
that residential property prices had fallen 50 per cent from their
September 2007 peak. Apartment prices were estimated to have
fallen 59 per cent from peak, while house prices had declined by
48 per cent.[22] But the statisticians at the CSO were measuring price
data for property purchases part financed by bank debt. And, by
2013, many property transactions were in cash and did not involve
bank debt. As mentioned in Chapter 3, a 2012 study by Goodbody
Stockbrokers, which analysed prices fetched at auctions, suggested
that sales prices there represented a 68 per cent price decline from
peak.[23]

Whatever the exact decline in property prices, there was
no doubting the sharp drop in the volume of property sales
taking place. It was estimated that the number of first-time-
buyer mortgages issued in 2012 was down by over three quarters
compared to 2007.[24] The very low volume of transactions combined
with another factor to produce a rise in Dublin property prices in
2013. That other factor was the failure of the banks to force the sale
of properties owned by delinquent borrowers in any significant
numbers. With the supply of houses for sale being constrained by
bank inaction, property prices were forced upwards. Evidence of
a lack of supply was the August 2013 report that 'four out of 10
houses sold in Dublin are executor sales following the death of the
owner, reflecting an acute shortage of houses for sale that is driving
prices up.'[25]

With the high number of mortgage arrears, one might have
expected a high number of properties to have been released onto

to the market as a result of repossessions. But the total number of repossession orders granted from 2007 to 2010 was less than 1,000, even though, by the end of 2010, there were 124,439 cases of mortgages being restructured or in arrears.[26] This slowness prompted the Central Bank to pressurise lenders to get to grips with the mortgage arrears crisis. Governor Patrick Honohan told an Oireachtas committee: 'Things are still not moving as quickly as the Central Bank would prefer; the indications are that the process is working, momentum is building, but there is some way to go.'[27]

But, for many, the fact that property prices were rising again was good news. By June 2013, Dublin property prices were 5 per cent above their August 2012 trough, while Dublin apartment prices were 14 per cent above their trough of the previous July. Had property prices reached a conclusive minimum in Ireland, or at least in Dublin? In August 2013, ESRI economist Dr David Duffy made a prediction for the year: 'I think there will be a rise in house prices in the order of 5–7 per cent nationally. Dublin will be 8–10 per cent.'[28] Duffy was making a brave prediction. But it wasn't the first time he had made a brave prediction. In November 2005, he had taken part in a public debate with Pam Woodall of *The Economist* magazine. She had argued that Irish house prices were then 'seriously overvalued'.[29] Duffy had pointed to demographic factors, significant levels of immigration, economic growth, employment growth and rising personal disposable income as the key drivers of the property market. He said that he expected these factors to remain positive over the next few years. In retrospect, it is clear that Woodall was right in 2005 and Duffy was wrong.

Signs that residential property prices were recovering were quietly welcomed by most property owners. For many it meant that the extent of negative equity might abate. For others, the danger of being trapped by negative equity at all might now disappear. For all property owners, it meant that their personal wealth might start to grow again after years of alarming decline. So it was understandable that news of rising property prices was greeted warmly by politicians, the media and many members of the general public. But was it reasonable to conclude that property prices had bottomed? I wonder.

Consider the contrast with property prices north of the border. Having 'enjoyed' a much greater property bubble in the Republic, for which we are suffering economically today, should we not therefore expect property prices in the Republic to suffer a larger peak-to-trough price fall than those north of the border? Yet Ulster Bank reported in August 2013 that residential property prices in Northern Ireland had declined by 66 per cent from peak.[30] This decline was reported in local currency (sterling) terms. But sterling had fallen by about 25 per cent against the euro since 2007. This would suggest that, in euro terms, residential prices had fallen over 72 per cent from peak in Northern Ireland.[31] That price fall is considerably in excess of the price fall suffered to date in the Republic. And it calls into question whether the 2013 rebound in residential property prices in Dublin will prove to be an enduring phenomenon.

An examination of rental yields available from commercial property investments raises the same uncomfortable question. Consider the sale of AIB Bankcentre in Ballsbridge, Dublin 4. This property came with a then government-guaranteed tenant with 14.5 years left to run on its rental contract. The annual rent was estimated by market observers to equal 9.6 per cent of the purchase price. This was at the high end of rental yields available for top quality commercial properties, which averaged 7–9 per cent at the time. But around the same time a house on the street where I live in Blackrock, Co. Dublin was sold for a price that would have generated a rental yield of just 5.5 per cent. Granted, this was at the lower end of the yields then available on residential property. But residential landlords face significant problems that commercial landlords don't face: they cannot offset all of their interest expense against their tax bill; and they face a greater danger that tenants will leave, refuse to pay or otherwise prove difficult to handle. As a result, one might expect rental yields on residential property to *exceed* those available on commercial property. The sale price fetched for the property on my road was not out of line with other sale prices in the area at the time.

The low rent yield for residential property compared to commercial property suggests that either commercial property or residential property is mispriced. Is it more likely that properties in the commercial sector, where there is a steady flow of transactions coupled with willing buyers and sellers, are mispriced, or is the problem in the residential sector, where transaction volumes have collapsed and there is an overhang of properties associated with non-performing loans? ECB data on the course of residential prices since 1990 provides final evidence that we should perhaps be cautious about the prospects for Irish house prices.[32] Looking at data since 1990 for Germany, Ireland, Spain and the eurozone as a whole shows three distinct phases: a period of convergence from 1990 to around 1995; a period of dramatic house price inflation for Ireland and Spain from 1995 to 2007; and a period of falling house prices for Ireland and Spain since 2008 (see Figure 4.2).

Figure 4.2: ECB *House Price Data Suggests Irish House Prices May Have Further to Fall*

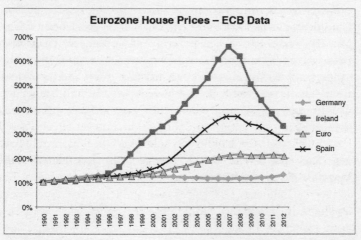

Source: Author's calculations based on ECB *data, available from: http://sdw.ecb.europa.eu, accessed January 2014.*

Normally when an asset price bubble deflates, prices don't merely return to the long-run norm; they fall below it, before eventually bottoming. Alarmingly, for those who argue that Irish residential property prices have put in an enduring bottom,

Irish residential property prices remain markedly above those in Germany and the eurozone average, if we take pre-eurozone prices as our base. Based on this data, it would appear that Irish residential prices have yet to return to their long-run norm, i.e. the eurozone average, never mind fall below it.

Wealth Effect

Whatever the future course of Irish residential property prices, their sharp fall over the 2008–12 period caused a heavy fall in the net wealth[33] of many Irish citizens and businesses. The problem for someone who had used financial debt to buy a property during the boom years was that their net wealth could be crushed. If the value of their property assets fell sharply while their financial debts remained largely unchanged, their net wealth could have been reduced to the point where they might have had negative equity, i.e. the value of their liabilities exceeded the value of their assets.

Researchers at the Irish Central Bank attempted to quantify this phenomenon in that body's quarterly bulletin, published in July 2011.[34] They estimated that, by the end of 2010, residential property prices had fallen by 35 per cent from their late 2006 levels. This change, combined with movements in other assets and liabilities, meant that the net wealth of Irish households and companies had fallen from €640 billion in 2006 to just €430 billion in 2010 (see Table 4.4).

Table 4.4: Fall in the Net Wealth of Irish Households and Companies from 2006 to 2010

	€ billions Q4 2006	€ billions Q4 2010	
Housing	€510	€330	-35%
Financial	€310	€300	
Total	€820	€630	
Debt	-€180	-€200	
Net	€640	€430	

Source: Mary Cussen and Gillian Phelan (2011), 'The Rise and Fall of Sectoral Net Wealth in Ireland', Central Bank Quarterly Bulletin Q2 2011, available from: http://financialregulator.ie, accessed January 2014, p. 73.

This estimated drop of €210 billion in net wealth was enormous. It represented about one third of Irish private sector wealth. More to the point, the drop equalled national economic output for over one and a half years.[35] While politicians and business representatives attempted to focus public attention on the modest good news concerning Ireland's annual income – for example, that economic growth was returning or that exports were performing strongly – the balance sheets of individuals were suffering. So there might have been economic growth of 1 or 2 per cent, but there were losses of over 150 per cent of annual income on many people's balance sheets.

The crushing of private wealth was probably the reason why the Irish savings rate rose so sharply during the crisis years. Politicians liked to imagine that this happened in response to budgetary uncertainty. It was thought that if only government could outline the difficult budgetary measures planned for the next few years, it could remove the uncertainty, reduce the savings rate and boost spending.

However, was it not more likely that people were reducing their spending because of what was happening to their personal balance sheets? Confronted with a situation where they were going to be poorer than they had originally envisaged, people had a simple but hard choice: reduce spending now and bring it into line with their reduced circumstances or keep spending at previous levels but risk running out of money much earlier than would be sensible.

The Central Bank calculations were based on a drop in housing asset values of 35 per cent. What if house prices dropped by 50 per cent, as they had by the end of 2012? Or what if prices converged on the eurozone average and dropped 70 per cent from peak? The impact on people's wealth, and thus the knock-on effects on spending, would have been even greater than they already were.

Bank Capital

Rising mortgage arrears and falling personal wealth both put huge pressure on the financial health of Ireland's banks. The banks faced threats from several directions.

First, customer losses threatened to become bank losses. Perhaps bank managers thought that when they sold the bulk of

their property and development loans to NAMA their position
would stabilise. But, if so, they had reckoned without large and
rising mortgage defaults. And they had also reckoned without big
problems in their loans to small and medium-sized enterprises
(SMEs). The increasing clamour for debt forgiveness and for debt
restructuring unsettled bankers. For, if the loan liabilities owed by
borrowers to banks were reduced, it would lead to an automatic
reduction in the loan assets owned by the banks. Too many loan
losses could increase the risk of bank insolvency by driving the
banks into negative equity.

An idea of the scale of the potential losses that might be lurking
in the banks' balance sheets can be gleaned from an examination
of their detailed financial statements. Financial statements require
banks to disclose details of their loan portfolios, including their
book value, and the banks' own estimates of the fair value of those
portfolios. As illustrated in Chapter 1, Table 1.1, the detailed figures
for Irish banks are alarming. As of December 2012, the book value
of the banks' loan books amounted to €197 billion. The banks' own
estimates of the fair value of their loan books at that date amounted
to €169 billion. So, by 2012, the Irish banks – which had proved
hopelessly optimistic in assessing their financial health at earlier
stages of the crisis – were effectively saying that the fair value of
their loans was €28 billion less than their carrying, book value. With
equity of just €23 billion, the Irish banks would face the threat of
immediate insolvency if they were to write down the book value of
their loans to their own estimates of fair value.

Second, even if the banks had no loan loss problem resulting
from their legacy portfolios, their underlying business models
looked broken. In 2012, the three main Irish banks – Bank of Ireland,
AIB and Permanent TSB – lost an aggregate €1.8 billion *before loan
loss provisions*. A significant element of this loss was caused by the
fees the Irish government charged the banks for guaranteeing their
liabilities under the Eligible Liabilities Guarantee (ELG) scheme.
This scheme ended in March 2013. But there were other major
problems standing in the way of a return to bank profitability. The
organisation and cost structures of the banks had been developed
in the boom years when 'selling' loans was the imperative. Now

the banks faced much smaller volumes of new lending business. Instead of selling loans, there was a huge requirement for analysing, managing and – in many cases – restructuring the loans that the banks had. Realigning the organisation of the banks from where it had been to where it now needs to go remains a major challenge for the management of the Irish banks.

Another major obstacle in the path of return to underlying profitability for Irish banks was the phenomenon of tracker mortgages. In the boom years the banks had issued large volumes of mortgage loans with interest rates tied to the ECB base rate. So, for example, a tracker mortgage might carry an interest charge of the ECB rate plus 1 per cent. At a time of easy access to cheap and plentiful liquidity, this practice seemed to make sense. But after 2008 it became harder and considerably more expensive for Irish banks to borrow money. The tracker mortgages became heavily loss-making. A tracker mortgage that charged a borrower the ECB rate plus 1 per cent had some logic when the banks were able to borrow money in the boom years for the ECB rate plus 0.5 per cent. But it had little logic if the banks now had to pay the ECB rate plus 2 per cent to borrow those funds. Such a scenario would mean that the bank was losing money on the loan at a rate of 1 per cent annually.

In July 2013 Merrion Stockbrokers estimated that tracker mortgages were costing Ireland's three domestic banks around €700 million every year.[36] In September 2013, it was reported that the ECB wanted the Irish government 'to phase out loss-making tracker mortgages over a five-year period in an effort to return the banks to profitability'.[37] In effect, this report could only mean that the ECB intended that either the Irish government or the holders of tracker mortgages would bear the cost of this measure. It was clear that the ECB didn't want to pick up the tab itself. However, it was also clear that the Irish government, whose own finances remained under pressure, was hardly able to pick up the tab. So, in effect, the ECB was suggesting that mortgage borrowers should pick up the tab 'in an effort to return the banks to profitability'. There was therefore little surprise when a Department of Finance spokesman said that the government was not considering the proposal.

But the very fact that such an extreme measure – the effective cancellation of the legal obligations that the banks had entered into regarding tracker mortgages – was being openly considered indicated the dire state of the Irish banking system. As renewed stress tests to examine whether Irish banks had sufficient equity capital loomed, Minister for Finance Michael Noonan said that he did not expect that the tests would result in the banks requiring extra capital to bolster their balance sheets.[38] Given the large gap between the banks' own estimates of their loans' fair value and their book value, his comments looked rather optimistic and were perhaps another example of the authorities understating the extent of Ireland's economic problems.

The Extent of Required Budgetary Austerity

The authorities have also been guilty of understating the extent of budgetary austerity that is likely to be necessary. As Budget 2014 approached in late 2013, the government wrestled with the size of the budgetary adjustment required: would it opt for adjustments of €3.1 billion, as originally intended, or of €2.5 billion, as the Labour Party wanted. But whatever the adjustment, the impression was conveyed that this was to be the second-last austerity budget.

As early as December 2012, Tánaiste Eamon Gilmore had argued that Ireland had achieved 85 per cent of its debt bailout targets and that the budget for 2013 'will therefore put the end in sight for this type of Budget'.[39] Another signal of a shift in the political tectonic plates came when the Secretary-General of the Department of Finance presented a paper the following August entitled 'Alternatives to Austerity'.[40] These calls became a clamour when the Chief Economist of the Irish Business and Employers' Confederation wrote that Budget 2014 must signal that an end to austerity was in sight.[41]

Was Eamon Gilmore correct in saying that, by 2013, Ireland had achieved 85 per cent of its debt bailout targets? He was correct in that 85 per cent of the austerity measures originally envisaged in the Troika's plan for Ireland had been implemented. That plan foresaw €33.1 billion of austerity measures. By 2013, €28 billion worth of measures (or 85 per cent of the planned total) had been implemented.

But Gilmore was quite incorrect in saying that Ireland had already traversed 85 per cent of its bitter austerity Calvary. Ireland wasn't just committed to reducing its General Government Deficit to 3 per cent of GDP as the Troika plan envisaged. Ireland was committed to going further. Under the so-called Stability Pact Treaty (Treaty on Stability, Coordination and Governance in the EMU), member states are also pledged to reduce their structural deficit to 0.5 per cent of GDP and to bring their national debt down to 60 per cent of GDP over 20 years. With GDP running at about €165, the gap between 3 per cent and 0.5 per cent of GDP exceeds €4 billion.

Another problem with Eamon Gilmore's estimate was that it didn't take into account that, as mentioned, €1 of budgetary adjustment measures do not translate into €1 of deficit reduction. So, between 2008 and 2013, Ireland had endured €28 billion of difficult austerity medicine. But the deficit had only reduced by a fraction of that amount. When, in May 2013, investment bankers JP Morgan estimated the extent of the austerity journey that various EU member states had travelled by the end of 2012, they reckoned that Ireland had gone 44 per cent of the way towards getting its debt down to 60 per cent of GDP over 20 years and just 26 per cent of the way towards getting its structural deficit down to 0.5 per cent of GDP.[42] So if, as many economists reckon, €2 of budgetary adjustments are required to achieve €1 of deficit reduction, further budgetary adjustments to the order of €8 billion may be required.

The irony was that, in late 2013, Ireland was looking forward to being the first patient in the eurozone ward to exit bailout, even though it had, at the time, the highest budget deficit in the entire EU.

Debt Sustainability

The general understanding of Ireland's economic crisis was that a credit and property bubble had popped in 2007, following which the Irish State struggled to cope with an extremely weak economy and an insolvent banking system. So, while thousands of households and corporations faced immense financial problems, the most visible focus in Ireland's bid for survival was the sustainability of our public debt level. For Ireland's public debt had to bear the impact of a sharply reduced economy, which meant reduced tax revenues and increased welfare spending, and bear the burden of bailing out the country's banking system. By the end of 2013 it was not completely clear that Ireland would be able to bear this burden.

The question of Ireland's debt sustainability does not centre on whether Ireland can repay its debt. Nor does it centre on whether Ireland can stop its debt continuing to grow. Rather, it centres on the relationship between Ireland's debt and its capacity to bear that debt. In most cases, figuring this out involves examining a country's debt-to-GDP ratio. For GDP is a key measure of annual national economic output. So, if Ireland could initially stabilise and then reduce its debt-to-GDP ratio, its capacity to service its debt would grow, and it would be less likely to be overwhelmed by the debt.

As we have already seen, the problem is that, in April 2013, the government's own watchdog, the Fiscal Advisory Council, warned that Ireland's debt load might not be sustainable.[43] This worrying position was echoed by the IMF in June 2013.[44] In November 2013 the government received another public warning from the Fiscal Advisory Council. It said 'very substantial risks' remained and, because of the easing off represented by Budget 2014, there was a 50 per cent chance key budgetary targets would be missed. The Fiscal Advisory Council further warned that the government would need a tougher budget in 2015 to meet the target if expected economic growth levels didn't materialise.[45]

There were other reasons to question Ireland's debt sustainability. Whereas it may, in most cases, make sense to compare a country's debt to its GDP, there are important reasons why it makes little sense in Ireland's case. That is primarily because Ireland's GDP is inflated by the profits which foreign multinationals make in the country.

Gross domestic product (GDP) uses a geographic approach to determine a country's national income. If something is made or produced in the country, the full value of that service or product goes into the country's GDP. So, if a microchip with a value of $100 is manufactured at Intel's Irish plant, the full $100 goes into Irish

GDP, even though $40 of that amount may be profits which will be claimed by Intel's, mainly American, shareholders. Gross national product (GNP), by contrast, uses an ownership approach when it comes to determining a country's national income. So, in the example above, only $60 (the $100 value of the chip minus that element of value attributable to non-national owners) would end up in Ireland's GNP.

For most countries, the difference between GDP and GNP is small. Most countries don't have ownership of substantial assets abroad which would boost GNP compared to GDP. Nor do most countries have large domestic assets which are owned by foreigners which would boost GDP over GNP – but Ireland does. As of 2012, Ireland's GDP exceeded its GNP by about 25 per cent. That meant that official measures of debt – comparing debt to GDP – were at risk of comparing Ireland's debt to an overstated measure of the country's capacity to bear that debt. Thus, Ireland's 2012 debt level of 117 per cent of GDP might appear tolerable in the context of other, similarly elevated, public debt levels across the eurozone periphery. But that level equalled 145 per cent of GNP, a figure that didn't feature much in public discussion of Ireland's debt problems.

It could be argued that large government cash balances – which had reached €124 billion by the end of 2012[46] – meant that Ireland's underlying debt problem was considerably smaller than the official gross debt figure implied. This was true. But it could equally be argued that there were even larger public liabilities which were not reflected in the official debt figures. The largest of these undeclared or unaccrued liabilities were public sector pensions and the liabilities built up by the Social Insurance Fund following its receipt of PRSI deductions from citizens. The combined size of these two liabilities was simply staggering.

The Comptroller and Auditor General estimated that the occupational pension liability which the State had built up in respect of public servants amounted to €116 billion by the end of 2009. In a report commissioned by the Department of Social Protection, accountants KPMG estimated that the present value of the projected shortfalls of the Social Insurance Fund totalled €324 billion at the end of 2010. So, depending on your choice of figures, you could honestly assert that Ireland's gross debt in 2012 was still large at 117 per cent of GDP. Or you could assert that Ireland's gross debt in 2012, including unaccrued liabilities, was a staggering 482 per cent of GNP.

Monetary Policy, Interest Rates and Money Supply

Monetary policy and interest rates, and their effect on money supply, have played the determinative part in Ireland's boom and bust. For, as mentioned, Ireland's boom was built on the following steps:

1. Ireland joined the eurozone.

2. Between 1997 and 2007, interest rates that were appropriate to the euro were inappropriately *low* for Ireland.

3. As a result, bank lending took off and the price of the main asset funded by bank lending – property – also took off.

Ireland's bust has represented the flip-side of the boom, with the key steps of the boom operating in reverse during the bust. Since 2008, interest rates that were appropriate for the eurozone as a whole have been inappropriately *high* for Ireland. As a result of this, and the absurdly high levels of debt and property prices reached by 2007, bank lending and property prices have collapsed.

Economists have formally estimated that ECB interest rates were too low for Ireland up to 2007 and too high for Ireland thereafter.[47] As we have already seen, in January 2005, Rossa White of Davy Stockbrokers estimated that Ireland should have a central bank interest rate of 6 per cent[48] – the ECB base rate at the time was just 2 per cent. Conversely, in May 2013, Dan McLaughlin of Bank of Ireland estimated that Ireland needed a Central Bank rate of -3.7 per cent at a time when the ECB base rate was +0.5 per cent. The ECB base rate swinging from a level where it was much too low for Ireland to one where it is much too high means that, in terms of credit, the Irish economy has taken a dangerous swing from binge-eating to crash dieting.

Annual rates of credit growth that reached 30 per cent in the boom years were replaced by a credit crunch in the bust. Instead of economic policy evening out the extremities of the business cycle, it grievously aggravated them. This matters enormously. Consider some remarks made in 2002 by perhaps the most important man on the planet when it comes to economic policy, Federal Reserve Chairman Ben S. Bernanke. He concluded his remarks at a conference honouring Milton Friedman on his ninetieth birthday with the words:

> *I would like to say to Milton and Anna: Regarding the Great Depression. You're right, we did it. We're very sorry. But thanks to you, we won't do it again.*[49]

Bernanke was confessing to Friedman and his co-author Anna Schwartz that it was the monetary policy mistakenly followed by the US Federal Reserve in the 1930s that made the Great Depression as damaging as it was. The problem was that the US Central Bank had allowed the American money supply to decline in the early 1930s. This, according to the monetary doctrine advanced by Friedman, was a catastrophic error. For, as Friedman concluded in his final publication, which appeared in 2006, 'What happens to the quantity of money has a determinative effect on what happens to national income.'[50]

Bernanke was apologising to Milton Friedman and Anna Schwartz for the failure of his responsibility, the US Federal Reserve, in allowing the US money supply to drop sharply in the years of the Great Depression. But an examination of Ireland's money supply figures since 2007 reveals an even sharper drop in Irish money supply than had occurred in the early years of the US Great Depression.

As of August 2013, M3, the broadest measure of Irish money supply, had dropped 20 per cent from its August 2007 peak. Four years into the Great Depression, in October 1933, US money supply had dropped 17 per cent from peak. Like Bernanke in 2002, will a future Governor of the Irish Central Bank apologise several decades from now for policy errors that caused the Irish people such suffering?

Exchange Rate

A country's exchange rate is its most important price. It determines the prices of imports and exports and it heavily influences a country's level of economic activity. Back in the days when Ireland still used the punt as its currency, close attention was paid to its exchange rate against sterling.

In December 2008, the punt rose above £1.20 sterling in value and nobody seemed to notice.[51] The reason for this was that, with the merging of the punt into the euro, we ceased to look carefully at the course of our exchange rate. But the competitive pressures facing Irish business had not changed after we joined the euro. And the sharp fall of sterling over 2007 and 2008 had made it considerably cheaper and our currency, the euro, considerably more expensive. But, because we had dismantled the punt–sterling currency thermometer when we joined the euro, we didn't really notice. The result was that, in addition to a property and credit crash in the domestic economy, Ireland suffered severe cost pressures compared to Britain.

Ireland's uncompetitive exchange rate compared to sterling in December 2008 illustrated a wider point. Locked into the euro, Ireland's real effective exchange rate (REER) had risen alarmingly since its original conversion rate was set in the summer of 1998. Years of interest rates that were set at an inappropriately low and inflationary level for Ireland had caused Ireland's costs to rise far more than the costs of its eurozone neighbours. Figure 4.3, which uses data from the Bank of International Settlements, compares the REER relative to Germany for a selection of eurozone member states. We can see that Ireland's REER rose by 29 per cent compared to Germany's between 1998 and 2007. Since then it has fallen back to a level where it is now 18 per cent higher. This means that Ireland's most important cost measure – the cost at which foreigners buy our goods and services – became incredibly high during the boom. And, during the bust, it has so far recovered only about one third of this deviation (see Figure 4.3).

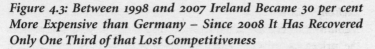

Figure 4.3: Between 1998 and 2007 Ireland Became 30 per cent More Expensive than Germany – Since 2008 It Has Recovered Only One Third of that Lost Competitiveness

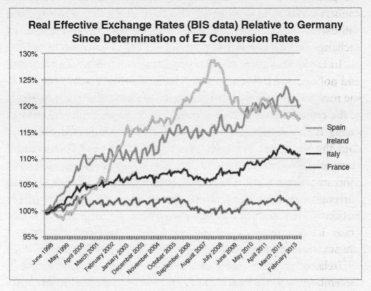

Source: *Based on data from the Bank of International Settlements, http://www.bis.org/statistics/ eer/, accessed January 2014.*

The situation is even worse in Spain. Spain's REER has grown even since 2007. And, relative to Germany, it currently shows a larger deviation than Ireland. A milder case of the same illness currently afflicts Italy. No such problem affects France. What this shows is that Ireland, Spain and probably Italy should never have joined the euro. The only ECB chief who argued against his country's membership of the euro was Italy's Antonio Fazio, Mario Draghi's predecessor as Governor of the Bank of Italy. Fabrizio Saccomanni, one of his senior officials, said of him, 'Although it is painful to admit for a central bank governor, Fazio felt that we had to devalue from time to time to regain competitiveness and to support economic activity.'[52] Saccomanni realised that Italy faced a simple choice: it could join the euro and enjoy the initial benefits of cheap finance but risk a lack of competitiveness and lack of economic growth later; or it could stick with the lira and retain the flexibility to devalue its currency in order to restore competitiveness and to reignite economic growth.

It is said that history doesn't repeat itself but that it does rhyme sometimes. An episode from economic history recalls the current problem Ireland and other countries on the eurozone periphery face as a result of an overvalued exchange rate. Winston Churchill was appointed Chancellor of the Exchequer in Britain in 1924. He decided to return sterling to the gold standard and the pre-World War I rate of exchange, even though Britain had, in the meantime, experienced considerable wartime inflation. The result was that Britain's REER was too high, its exports were too expensive and domestic demand weakened. This unleashed economic deflation. It also prompted the economist John Maynard Keynes to draft a sharply critical polemic, 'The Economic Consequences of Mr Churchill'. In a key passage Keynes wrote:

> He [Churchill] was just asking for trouble. For he was committing himself to force down money-wages and all money-values, without any idea how it was to be done. Why did he do such a silly thing? Partly, perhaps, because he has no instinctive judgment to prevent him from making mistakes; partly because, lacking this instinctive judgment, he was deafened by the clamorous voices of conventional finance; and, most of all, because he was gravely misled by his experts.[53]

Churchill later regarded this as the greatest mistake of his life. The decision caused economic deflation, unemployment, human misery and the Great Strike of 1926. It wasn't until 1931, under pressure from financial markets, that Britain finally reversed this decision.

WHAT MIGHT THE ECONOMIC MASTERS SUGGEST?
A telling aspect of Irish political and economic debate during the crisis has been how seldom the lessons of the great economic masters have featured. Keynes wrote his pamphlet criticising British exchange rate policy in 1925. He had also written an

earlier pamphlet, in 1919, criticising the savage post-World War I settlement which the Allies had imposed on Germany. In that earlier document he wrote the following passage, the relevance of which can be applied nearly a century later to the EU's treatment of Greece:

> The policy of reducing Germany to servitude for a generation, of degrading the lives of millions of human beings, and of depriving a whole nation of happiness should be abhorrent and detestable, even if it were possible, even if it enriched ourselves, even if it did not sow the decay of the whole civilised life of Europe.[54]

Despite the direct relevance of what Keynes and others had to say, their lessons hardly feature in Irish public debate. Perhaps this is because, as the historian Joe Lee acidly commented, Irish public discourse is more 'sub-intellectual than anti-intellectual. Anti-intellectualism is too intellectually demanding.'[55] But what insights do economic theory and the economic masters have to offer Ireland?

John Maynard Keynes

John Maynard Keynes (1883–1946) was the most influential economist of the twentieth century. He argued that markets could not, on their own, be relied upon to operate in a satisfactory manner. His conclusion was that state intervention was necessary to moderate 'boom and bust' cycles of economic activity. Keynes's magnum opus, *The General Theory of Employment, Interest and Money*, was published in 1936. This work disputes the earlier neoclassical economic model, which held that, left to its own devices, the market would naturally generate full employment. Keynes argues that because of price stickiness – the fact that workers often refuse to lower their wages even if a classical economist might argue that they should – high unemployment can occur. This means that deflation would lead to rising real wages and falling employment and output.

Keynes's General Theory argues that demand, not supply, is the key variable governing the overall level of economic activity. If a deflationary shock hits an economy – for example, as a result of an asset bubble bursting – unemployment and unused production capacity will result. The danger is that households and corporations will react to asset price falls and the resulting drop in economic activity by cutting back and by attempting to increase their savings. However, if everybody attempts to increase their savings at the same time, there will be a sharp drop in consumption and demand. This may cause further drops in the value of assets and more intensive attempts to save. A downward spiral of asset prices and economic activity may result. This happened in the Great Depression during the 1930s. What is rational for the individual – to attempt to increase saving in response to diminished economic circumstances – can be irrational for an entire society. This is called 'the paradox of thrift'. The Keynesian remedy is for the State to borrow so that the private sector can save. This was very well described by Paul McCulley and Zoltan Pozsar:

> Deleveraging can be rational for an individual household. It can be rational for an individual corporation. It can be rational for an individual country. However, in the aggregate it begets the paradox of thrift: what is rational at the microeconomic level is irrational at the community, or macroeconomic, level.
>
> This is not to say that the private sector should not deleverage. It has to. It is a part of the economy's healing process and a necessary first step toward a self-sustaining economic recovery.
>
> However, deleveraging is a beast of a burden that capitalism cannot bear alone. At the macro level, deleveraging must be a managed process: for the private sector to deleverage without causing a depression, the public sector has to move in the opposite direction and re-lever by effectively viewing the balance sheets of the monetary and fiscal authorities as a consolidated whole.[56]

So Keynes broke from orthodoxy in denying that markets self-regulate in a satisfactory way. Instead, he advocated government spending deficits as a policy tool to sustain economic activity in a severe economic downturn. The fact that, across the globe, countries are still running large spending deficits in 2013, five years since this crisis first broke, indicates that Keynesianism is now government orthodoxy.

The central problem for Ireland is that not only is the indebtedness of the Irish State extraordinarily high compared to that of other states, but that picture is replicated for the Irish household and business sectors. In its March 2012 *Macro Financial Review,* the Irish Central Bank depicted the position for Irish household debt (see Figure 4.4).

Figure 4.4: Irish Household Debt is Enormous in Relative Terms

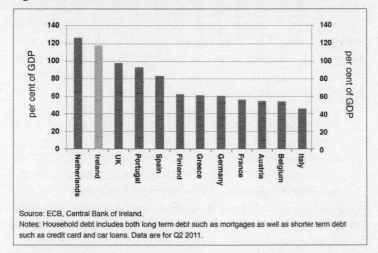

Source: ECB, Central Bank of Ireland.
Notes: Household debt includes both long term debt such as mortgages as well as shorter term debt such as credit card and car loans. Data are for Q2 2011.

Source: Irish Central Bank (2012), 'Macro Financial Review', available from: http://centralbank. ie, accessed January 2014, p. 15.

It also depicted the comparative position for Irish corporate debt (see Figure 4.5).

Figure 4.5: Irish Corporate Debt is Also Enormous in Relative Terms

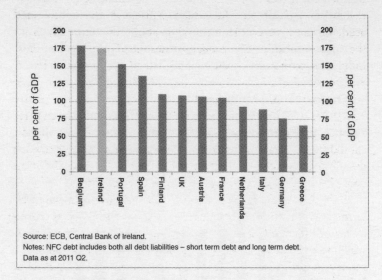

Source: ECB, Central Bank of Ireland.
Notes: NFC debt includes both all debt liabilities – short term debt and long term debt.
Data as at 2011 Q2.

*Source: Irish Central Bank (2012), 'Macro Financial Review', available from: http://centralbank.
ie, accessed January 2014, p. 8.6.*

In each case, Irish debt levels were compared to GDP. Had they been compared to GNP, as in my firm opinion they should have been, the resulting debt level would have appeared approximately 25 per cent greater.

In 2011, economists Dermot O'Leary and Don Walshe studied the question of whether Ireland's plan – to simultaneously reduce private debt, bank debt and government borrowing – made economic sense. They reached a worrying conclusion:

> *Ireland wants to reach a destination whereby it will have a smaller private debt level, a smaller banking system and stable public finances. That is the story of stocks. How it gets there, outside of default, is determined by flows. This paper shows that the current policy course is inconsistent with the achievement of all three goals in a reasonable timeframe and sustainable way.*[57]

Milton Friedman

Milton Friedman (1912–2006) led the intellectual counter-revolution against the Keynesian consensus that dominated academic and government thinking about the economy from the 1950s onwards. *The Economist* described him as 'the most influential economist of the second half of the 20th century ... possibly of all of it.'[58]

Friedman was the main intellectual proponent of monetarism. This holds that there is a close and stable association between price inflation and the money supply. It proposes that price inflation should be regulated with monetary deflation and price deflation with monetary inflation. He famously quipped that price deflation could be fought by 'dropping money out of a helicopter'.[59]

Friedman wrote extensively on the Great Depression, which he termed the Great Contraction. He argued that it had been caused by an ordinary financial shock, the duration and seriousness of which were greatly increased by the subsequent contraction of the money supply caused by the misguided policies of the US Federal Reserve. The problem for Ireland was that, by 2013, the country had endured several years of its money supply contracting.

Bottom Line

Since we are locked into the euro, the remedies proposed by both Keynes and Friedman cannot be applied in Ireland.

T.K. WHITAKER'S WISE WORDS

Whether we consider mortgage arrears, bank lending, property prices, the effects of crushed wealth positions, bank capital, the extent of budgetary austerity, the sustainability of Ireland's debts, monetary policy or Ireland's real effective exchange rate, one thing is clear: the authorities have been seriously understating the extent of Ireland's problems. This would not be the first time that the Irish authorities deliberately downplayed a crisis for fear of scaring the public, as this comment from a leading public servant reveals:

> *The economic situation is more serious than we have been admitting officially. We have deliberately not been too pessimistic*

*in public for fear of undermining confidence and also in the hope
that as the months went by things would show a sufficient turn
for the better. This hope is not being realised – indeed, it was
not soundly based – and we now have to increase the corrective
measures. We should also, without being alarmist, be more
forthright about the nature and extent of our problems. We
would be deluding ourselves if we continued to make reassuring
comments on their temporary nature.... There is a basic difficulty
of a more lasting character and it is time we did something more
effective about it.*[60]

This remark was made by T.K. Whitaker in October 1965.
The then Secretary of the Department of Finance was later voted
'Irishman of the 20th Century' for his pivotal role in the country's
economic development. Even though Whitaker made the remark
to describe the official reaction to a foreign exchange crisis that
occurred several decades ago, it describes perfectly the official
response to the current crisis: the authorities 'have deliberately not
been too pessimistic in public for fear of undermining confidence';
they should 'be more forthright about the nature and extent of our
problems'; there 'is a basic difficulty of a more lasting character';
and 'it is time we did something more effective about it.'

It is time we considered Plan B.

05 PLAN B

*More than any other time in history,
mankind faces a crossroads. One path
leads to despair and utter hopelessness.
The other, to total extinction. Let us pray
we have the wisdom to choose correctly.*

Woody Allen

IRELAND NEEDS PLAN B

We cannot carry the level of debt that we have when the economy is showing so little growth. Indeed, that high debt level is a key reason why the economy is showing so little growth. By making interest rate cuts and extending the maturity of many loans, our creditors have already tacitly admitted the unsustainability of Ireland's debt levels.

We also need to exit the eurozone. Continued membership of it is another key reason for Ireland's parlous rate of economic growth. For it denies us the aggressive monetary policy that we need, a policy currently being followed in the US, Britain and Japan. And it inflicts on us a currency level and cost levels which, in international terms, are too high. They could be put right instantaneously with a substantial currency devaluation – but that is only possible outside the euro. Or they can be put right with a very prolonged period of domestic austerity that contains cost growth here while costs grow abroad. This could take decades and is what we condemn ourselves to while we remain within the euro. But what are the detailed implications of default and eurozone exit?

THE IMPLICATIONS OF DEFAULT

For Ireland to suspend payment of its debts while seeking their restructuring would be a grave step. For it would be an admission that Ireland was not able to pay its way internationally and to repay debts freely entered into. Although an Irish default would come as a surprise, sovereign defaults are actually quite common. Some countries have spent a large part of their history in default. Spain has spent over 20 per cent of its existence in default; Greece around 50 per cent.[1]

Legal Implications of Default

Historically, sovereign debt was not subject to normal bankruptcy law. However, US and British legislation passed in the 1970s has diluted this legal immunity. Since then, there have been several cases where creditors have used legal avenues to seek payment from governments that have defaulted on their debts. For example, in October 2012, an Argentine naval vessel crewed by more than 200 sailors was seized in Ghana as part of efforts by US hedge fund Elliott Capital Management to collect on government bonds on which Argentina had defaulted in 2001.[2] The effect of this legal change since the 1970s has been to complicate and, in some cases, slow down the process of restructuring sovereign debt. If the debt is largely held domestically, then national law-makers will play a key role in how matters are resolved. But if the debt is largely held by foreign creditors, then they and their governments can exercise significant influence over how a debt crisis is resolved. As most of Ireland's debt is held by foreign creditors based in the EU, an Irish debt default may therefore lead to strained relations with the EU.

A complicating factor is that government debt defaults tend to cluster, i.e. when one default occurs, it can be rapidly followed by others. In the words of the economic research company Capital Economics: 'Rather like London buses, defaults tend to arrive in groups.'[3] Given the similarity and scale of the economic crisis being suffered across the eurozone periphery, it is therefore unlikely that Ireland would be in default on its own for long. As of the end of 2013, Greece and Portugal have debt levels that are seen by David Marsh, the author of the definitive histories of both the Bundesbank and the euro, as unsustainable:

*It is well-nigh inevitable that Greece and Portugal, the two most
exposed countries in economic and monetary union (EMU), with
government debt projected by the OECD at 181% and 132% of
gross domestic product respectively next year, will need a formal
debt write-down in 2014 – where Germany will foot the largest
slice of the bill.*[4]

As of the end of 2013, Ireland's public debt is budgeted to reach
124 per cent of GDP or, more significantly, 155 per cent of GNP.
So an Irish debt default or debt restructuring is, in my opinion,
inevitable. It is also questionable whether the debt levels of Spain
and Italy are sustainable. And some form of default or restructuring
also appears inevitable for several other eurozone countries. Ireland
would have some safety in numbers in negotiating the terms of its
debt restructuring.

But there can often be a substantial delay between debt default
and a final agreement on debt restructuring. Russia was able to
restructure its debts in 2000 just two years after it defaulted in 1998.
But Latin American countries that defaulted in the 1980s had to
wait over a decade, on average, before their debts were conclusively
restructured.

The Costs of Default
In a July 2011 study of sovereign defaults, Capital Economics
identified six costs of default:[5]

1. *Loss of market access for the sovereign and/or higher future
   sovereign borrowing costs.* In the short-run, the Irish government
   would be unable to borrow in the immediate wake of a default.
   In the longer-run, once it was able to access debt markets again,
   the Irish government would probably have to pay a higher
   rate of interest on its borrowings. A 2006 study by economists
   at the Bank of England found that countries that defaulted
   between 1970 and 2000 paid higher interest rates and had lower
   credit ratings in 2003–5 than countries with the same debt-to-
   GDP ratios that had not defaulted.[6] But, as of 2014, the Irish
   government will only be borrowing money to pay off interest
   on old debts. It budgets on running a primary surplus and

therefore should not need to borrow money to fund day-to-day or investment spending.

And markets appear to have short memories. A different study by the IMF found that credit ratings between 1999 and 2002 were affected only by defaults since 1995.[7] It was found that defaults appear to have no significant effect on interest rates after the second year.

2. *Loss of market access for the private sector.* Foreign lenders may not make a large distinction between Irish public and private sector borrowers if the Irish government was to default on its debts, and they may deny fresh funding to any Irish borrower. Another IMF study found that defaults lead to a 40 per cent decline in foreign credit to private companies in the defaulting country.[8] With Ireland's slow-motion banking crisis, this decline may have already happened in Ireland. Foreign banks (Halifax Bank of Scotland, Ulster Bank, Danske Bank, Rabobank, etc.) have already sharply curtailed their activities in Ireland.

3. *Negative political consequences for relationships with creditor governments.* It is unlikely that Ireland's eurozone and EU partners would welcome an Irish eurozone exit. Nor would the US welcome it. Our EU partners may even be tempted to punish Ireland. That was the initial reaction of Jean-Claude Trichet to Denmark's June 1992 vote against the Maastricht Treaty. Then a senior official with the French Treasury, Trichet told the European Monetary Committee that the other EU countries should proceed anyway and that Denmark 'should be punished for its foolishness'.[9] So there might be big political problems, at least initially. And they could persist for some time, perhaps for as long as 18–24 months. But does the EU wish to get smaller and expel Ireland? No. Does the EU wish to have its business permanently disrupted by arguments over the debts of Ireland and other defaulting member states? No. In addition, there are several steps which Ireland could take to soften any blow to relations with the EU: pre-warn, co-ordinate planning, attempt to remain within the law and declare our firm desire to stay within the EU.

4. *Banking crisis, capital flight and a currency crisis.* Elements of these problems have already occurred in Ireland but their effect has been mitigated by the availability of emergency ECB funding. But, in mid-2011, the ECB became more and more reluctant to advance any additional finance, which forced Ireland into the hands of the Troika. The same thing happened to Cyprus in March 2013.

5. *Losses for domestic bond holders.* As of September 2013, investors resident in Ireland, mainly the Irish Central Bank and commercial banks, owned Irish government bonds with a total nominal value of over €50 billion. If Irish debt was to suffer a 40 per cent haircut or write-down in value, that would trigger losses of over €20 billion for those domestic investors. Roger Bootle has estimated that the losses resulting from a 50 per cent reduction in the value of Irish government bonds would cost Irish banks 41 per cent of their equity.[10]

6. *Domestic political costs to the government.* The drop in political popularity suffered by the Brian Cowen-led government when it was forced to call in the Troika was sharp and clear. This gives a sense of the political losses that would probably be triggered by default and eurozone exit for whichever parties were in government at the time.

The Economic Impact of Default

A survey of sovereign defaults by *The Economist* reported that 'Sovereign defaults do not typically lead to economic catastrophe.'[11] Another article in that magazine reported that – for selected defaults after 1999 – annual economic growth rates were more than 2 per cent higher in the five years after default compared to the five years leading up to default.[12]

Historically, sovereign default has often proven to be a good thing for the country concerned, as it can set the stage for economic recovery. Benefits to the defaulting country are likely to be greater if the default is accompanied by a substantial debt write-off, if it is followed by currency depreciation and if global economic conditions are reasonably positive.

Capital Economics concluded its study of sovereign default
by suggesting that defaulting eurozone states should also strongly
consider dumping the euro:

> *In this situation, we think governments in peripheral euro-zone
> countries may eventually be forced to consider leaving the euro.
> Default without devaluation may simply prolong the agony. Even if
> the politicians are very reluctant to do so, the population may force
> the issue through political protests and/or moving their savings out
> of the banks. Indeed, we think a decision to leave the euro may
> ultimately be the best solution for some countries, as it would in the
> long run create the conditions for a strong, export-led recovery.*[13]

Examples of Past Defaults Coupled with Currency Devaluations

Before 1997, East Asia was booming. From 1993 to 1996, the nine
major East Asian countries – China, Hong Kong, Indonesia, Korea,
Malaysia, the Philippines, Singapore, Taiwan and Thailand –
averaged annual GDP growth of over 6 per cent each year. This
spurred huge capital inflows from abroad, which led to property
and stock market bubbles coupled with a dependency on foreign
capital. Unfortunately for the countries of East Asia, almost all their
borrowing was short term in nature and much of it was in foreign
currency. This created a currency mismatch as investors financed
domestic investments with foreign currency borrowing. There was
also a maturity mismatch as assets were often longer term and
illiquid (i.e. difficult to sell quickly), while liabilities were typically
short term and liquid (i.e. could be demanded back quickly).
Then, in the summer of 1997, several Korean conglomerates went
bankrupt. This triggered a crisis that reached across the whole
globe. Right up to the crisis, almost all Asian leaders had denied
that the currencies would be devalued. But, during the summer,
the Thai baht, the Indonesian rupiah and the South Korean won
were all devalued, and there were many major debt defaults.

After this crisis, South Korea and Thailand experienced sharp
downturns, but then their economies grew quickly for the following
decade and they recovered their pre-crisis GDP levels within two
and three years respectively. By 2001, Thailand's economy had

recovered. The increasing tax revenues allowed the country to balance its budget and repay its debts to the IMF in 2003, four years ahead of schedule.

These experiences contrasted with the experience of Hong Kong, which opted not to devalue its currency but to maintain its fixed rate of exchange with the US dollar. Hong Kong's economy did not see GDP make a full recovery until 2005. In his study on the Asian crisis, Michael B. Devereux from British Columbia University contrasted the experience of Singapore with its floating exchange rate and Hong Kong with its fixed exchange rate. He found that the slow recovery of output growth in Hong Kong relative to Singapore post-1997 could be largely explained by Hong Kong's fixed exchange rate.[14]

The success of the East Asian countries that defaulted and devalued in 1998 was echoed by Argentina when it was forced to do the same in 2001–2. This experience was analysed in a study by the Center for Economic and Policy Research:

Argentina was trapped in a severe recession from mid-1998 to the end of 2001. Attempts to stabilize the economy and maintain the currency peg to the U.S. dollar, through monetary and fiscal tightening, led by the IMF and backed by tens of billions of dollars in lending, failed to arrest the economy's downward spiral.

In December of 2001, the government defaulted on its debt, and a few weeks later it abandoned the currency peg to the dollar. The default and devaluation contributed to a severe financial crisis and a sharp economic contraction, with GDP shrinking by about 5 percent in the first quarter of 2002. However, recovery began after that one quarter of contraction, and continued until the world economic slowdown and recession of 2008–2009. The economy then rebounded, and the IMF now projects growth of 8 percent for 2011.[15]

Their main finding was astonishing:

The Argentine economy has grown 94 percent for the years 2002–2011, using International Monetary Fund (IMF) projections for the end of this year. This is the fastest growth in the Western

Hemisphere for this period, and among the highest growth rates in the world.[16]

Another study found that few of the feared penalties for defaulting actually transpired. In effect, Argentina got away with it.

We show that the Argentine case contradicts many of their standard predictions, in particular its posterior lack of access to international credit, restriction to international trade and negative economic growth. Moreover, it corroborates the historical fact that many defaulters 'get away with it'.[17]

The lessons from history are clear. Whether it is East Asia in 1997, Argentina in 2002 or earlier episodes, the broad story is the same. People are told that unsustainable debts must be sustained and that there is no alternative. Severe recession and human suffering result. Apocalyptic warnings frighten people from considering the alternative course of action: default and devaluation. Years later, when it is clear that default and devaluation delivered the country from crisis, people wonder what all the fuss was about and how such a wrong-headed policy could have been sustained by so many clever people for so long.

THE IMPLICATIONS OF CURRENCY EXIT

The Key Arguments for Eurozone Exit

The main arguments for exiting the eurozone can be summarised as follows:

1. The euro should never have been introduced as its members' economies are too dissimilar for a common monetary policy to function effectively.

2. The main result of the eurozone's flaws – inappropriate monetary policy – has caused Ireland to swing from economic binge eating to economic crash dieting. From 1997 to 2007, inappropriately low interest rates triggered credit, property and cost booms as well as a boom in domestic activity levels. Since 2008, the debt legacy of the boom years, coupled

with inappropriately high interest rates, has led to severe
downward pressure on credit, property prices and costs, while
economic activity levels have plunged to those of an economic
depression.

3. Continued membership of the eurozone means that Ireland
    is denied the appropriate monetary policy (i.e. aggressive
    quantitative easing as practised in the US, Britain, Japan,
    etc.) and the currency devaluation required to restore
    competitiveness and escape depression.

4. Even if all of the economic imbalances unleashed by the
    eurozone – generations and nations condemned to penury
    and unemployment, unsustainable levels of public debt,
    unmanageable mountains of private debt, and broken banking
    systems – could be reversed, the fundamental flaw at the root
    of the eurozone – interest rates that are gravely inappropriate
    for national circumstances – would *guarantee* that similar
    imbalances would build again in the future.

Examples of Previous Exits from Currency Zones

Andrew K. Rose, Professor of International Business at the
University of California, Berkeley, carried out a study of over 130
countries that exited currency union between 1946 and 2005. In
some cases studied by Rose, small colonies were exiting currency
areas. In other cases, large countries were breaking up or leaving a
common currency. The study's central conclusion was remarkably
reassuring: 'I find…there is remarkably little macroeconomic
volatility around the time of currency union dissolutions.'[18]

Three examples of monetary unions that have some parallels
with the eurozone are the Austro-Hungarian Empire, the Russian
rouble zone and the Czech–Slovak monetary union. Each of these
contained sovereign countries that shared a single currency for a
while after the political dissolution of a state. The sovereign states
then adopted their own currencies, thus breaking up the currency
union. The most recent break-up was that which followed the
dissolution of Czechoslovakia into the Czech Republic and
Slovakia. British MEP Daniel Hannan asked a Slovakian economist

how his country had managed the transition. 'Very easily,' he replied, before adding:

> One Friday, after the markets had closed, the head of our central bank phoned round all the banks and told them that, over the weekend, someone from his office would come round with a stamp to put on all their banknotes, and that, until the new notes and coins came into production, those stamped notes would be Slovakia's legal tender. On the Monday morning, we had a new currency.[19]

This was not the first time that the citizens of the two Central European countries had experienced the dissolution of a currency union. For both countries were part of the Austro-Hungarian Empire, which broke up in the wake of its 1918 defeat in World War I. Peter Garber and Michael Spencer produced a detailed account of the break-up of the Austro-Hungarian currency union in 1919, concluding that it provides several important lessons for today:

> This episode suggests five lessons for currency reform elsewhere. First, currency separation can be accomplished relatively quickly. It involves little more than marking banknotes circulating within the breakaway state with a stamp. This initial operation will necessarily be followed by an exchange of stamped notes for new national currency, but it buys time for the authorities to plan the second stage carefully. Second, the exchange of old notes for new provides an opportunity for the authorities to eliminate any 'monetary overhang' by imposing a tax on notes exchanged. Such a tax was imposed in the Serbo-Croat-Slovene State, Czechoslovakia, and Hungary. Third, if currency reforms are not conducted simultaneously throughout the former currency union, differential conversion rates for the old currency will create incentives for individuals to spend or exchange their old notes in the region where they are most valuable. The imposition of a tax, or differential expected rates of inflation, creates another incentive to move notes to escape the tax. Thus old notes will flow into those countries with the most favourable tax-inclusive real conversion rate. Fourth,

states that are late in breaking away from the currency union may find more than their share of the stock of old notes dumped on them. Breakaway reforms elsewhere may cause people to sell their old notes for goods and assets in those states where they are still legal tender. The last to convert the old notes will then absorb both the notes originally circulating in its territories and many of the notes previously circulating elsewhere. A liquidation of old central bank assets prorated on the amount of currency collected will only partially compensate for lost goods. Finally, currency reform will succeed in creating a stable medium of exchange only if it is accompanied by sound fiscal and monetary policies.[20]

These examples highlight a number of important lessons for any possible eurozone break-up. They highlight the fact that capital flows have, on several occasions, forced governments to introduce a new currency sooner than they had planned, for example, in Latvia in 1992 and in the Czech and Slovak Republics in 1993. They also suggest that countries will need to restrict the right to withdraw money from bank accounts. Countries may also need to introduce capital controls to prevent capital flight or excessive inflows of currency seeking to benefit from redenomination and currency appreciation – this theme will be examined presently. They also give pointers on the detailed mechanics of creating a new currency.

Which Eurozone Members Have the Greatest Incentive to Exit?

In July 2012 the analysts at Bank of America, Merrill Lynch, prepared a study examining which of the 11 eurozone members studied had the greatest relative incentive to exit the common currency area.[21] They examined this question from a number of perspectives.

First, the study looked at a country's ability to conduct an orderly exit. In large part, this depends on whether a country is dependent on external finance to fund imports and government. Countries running a current account surplus, i.e. their exports exceed their imports, and a government surplus, i.e. government revenues exceed expenses, are less dependent on external financing and would be more able to execute an orderly eurozone exit. In terms of its ability to carry out an orderly exit from the eurozone,

Germany ranked first, while Ireland ranked ninth out of 11, with only Greece and Spain ranking behind it.

The study next examined the impact of eurozone exit on each country's economic growth prospects. This would depend, in large part, on (a) the degree of currency devaluation experienced following exit; (b) the impact of the currency move on exports; and (c) other factors which might constrain export growth. In terms of the expected impact on economic growth as a result of leaving the eurozone, Ireland ranked first. Germany ranked last, as its currency would probably increase in value and thus dampen exports and economic growth.

The study also looked at the implications for countries' borrowing costs. Within the eurozone, peripheral countries face high bond yields, in part because they lack independent monetary policy and an independent currency. This reinforces perceived devaluation risk and default risk, thus pushing up borrowing costs. On this score, Greece would benefit most from eurozone exit, Germany would benefit least and Ireland would enjoy the third highest benefits among the 11 countries surveyed.

Finally, the authors attempted to predict the impact of eurozone exit on the balance sheets of households, businesses, banks and the government as a result of existing cross-border holdings. This was based on the expectation that exiting countries would redenominate their external euro liabilities into their new currency, e.g. into, let us say, the new drachma or punt nua (new punt). If these new currencies were to devalue, this denomination would achieve a reduction in the real value of liabilities, thus leading to an improvement in the balance sheets of the countries affected. On this score, Ireland was expected to benefit more than any other country, while Germany would be the biggest loser.

In their overall assessment of these factors, the authors of the study stated:

> It is not our intention to downplay the costs of any exit (orderly or disorderly). However, as the crisis deepens and with more and more policy options unimaginable two years ago finding their way to the table, our framework allows investors to understand the

cost–benefit considerations of an exit as part of the policy reaction
functions of different countries.[22]

They then concluded that 'while Germany and Austria have the
least incentive of any eurozone countries to exit, Italy and Ireland
have the most.'

THE MAIN ELEMENTS OF PLAN B
Before going into the steps Ireland would need to take to exit
the eurozone, let us take a look at the general background and
challenges to eurozone exit and currency redenomination.

The Challenges of Eurozone Exit
Several immense challenges – including technical, legal, political
and moral challenges – confront those who argue in favour of any
member state exiting the eurozone:

- Redenomination of financial assets and liabilities within any
  exiting eurozone member state.

- Whether and how to redenominate cross-border contracts
  denominated in euro, if one party to the contract is resident in
  a member state exiting the eurozone.

- How to avoid damaging bank runs and capital flight from a
  wobbling eurozone member in advance of its eurozone exit.

- The link between exit from EMU and sovereign debt
  restructuring.

- How to avoid the damaging knock-on effects of eurozone exit
  and debt restructuring on the part of peripheral eurozone
  members on the banks and public finances of core eurozone
  members.

- How to avoid a wider financial contagion that could have
  global reach.

- How to manage bruised political relations within the EU
  following the partial (or total) fracturing of the eurozone.

- How to manage the multiple legal implications of eurozone
  exit.

At the root of many of the challenges posed above lies the mathematics of currency redenomination.

The Mathematics of Currency Redenomination

Under the *lex monetae* principle, every sovereign state has the right to determine the default currency in which domestic financial transactions within its territory will be carried out.[23] Before 2002, the default currency in Ireland was the punt; afterwards it was the euro. The changeover from punt to euro took place as a result of treaties ratified and legislation passed by the Oireachtas. This allowed the authorities to require that all domestic financial assets and liabilities within the State denominated in punts be redenominated into euros at the official translation rate of IR£1 = €1.27.

So it was that on 1 January 1999, all punt financial balances – company debt, mortgage debt, invoices outstanding, government debt – became euro financial balances. The same process of redenomination applied to continuing contractual obligations and prices. So pay rates, salary levels, welfare rates, shop prices and even the cost of a Big Mac all moved in lockstep from punts into euros at the rate of IR£1 = €1.27.

But it is highly unlikely that reversing this process – and switching from the euro to the punt nua – would flow nearly as smoothly. Whereas there was a lengthy period of preparation for the switchover to the euro, there would be little or no time to prepare for the switch out of the euro. Second, and more importantly, the switch out of the euro would probably be accompanied by significant currency devaluation. This would likely produce very significant economic consequences that, for many, could lead to bankruptcy.

Let us consider the possible economic consequences of currency redenomination accompanied by significant currency devaluation. Suppose there are two friends, Fast Eddie and Thick Tim. Fast Eddie is the archetypal 'cute hoor': amoral, unscrupulous and profitable in nearly everything he does. His sidekick, Thick Tim, enjoys the whiff of sulphur he gets from accompanying Eddie. But he's not blessed with Eddie's insights or his ruthlessness and he often picks up the wrong end of the stick when it comes to important matters. As a result of drinking in the right pubs in the right part of Dublin where top public servants let their hair down, Eddie learns on a Wednesday that Ireland plans to exit the euro that weekend. The next day, he goes to his old banker friend, Jimmy, in Dublin and he borrows €1 million. He has these funds wired to Belfast where he deposits the funds. Despite having everything carefully explained to him, Thick Tim does the exact opposite: he borrows €1 million in Belfast and he deposits it in Dublin. As a result of these transactions, both Eddie and Tim have apparently fully hedged positions, where their assets and liabilities offset one another exactly, as they enter the weekend (see Table 5.1).

Table 5.1: Both Eddie and Tim Have Apparently Fully Hedged Positions

Friday	Fast Eddie	Thick Tim
Dublin	-€1,000,000	+€1,000,000
Belfast	+€1,000,000	-€1,000,000
Net position	€0	€0

Then, over the weekend, the government announces that Ireland is leaving the euro with immediate effect. For the sake of simplicity, old euro balances within the State will be redenominated into punt nua at a rate of 1:1, i.e. €1 = NIR£1. Now the positions of Eddie and Tim are as shown in Table 5.2.

Table 5.2: Positions of Eddie and Tim Once Ireland Leaves the Euro

Weekend	Fast Eddie	Thick Tim
Dublin	-NIR£1,000,000	+NIR£1,000,000
Belfast	+€1,000,000	-€1,000,000

In Dublin, the financial positions of Eddie and Tim have changed into punt nua (using the symbol NIR£). But their

positions in Belfast remain unchanged. For they entered financial
positions in Belfast in a currency that still exists, even if Ireland and
some other European countries no longer use that currency, under
contracts governed by the laws of Belfast and the United Kingdom.
The fact that financial positions south of the border would face
wholesale change would have no effect on the contractual or legal
position north of the border. So euro balances in Belfast or London
would remain just that, euro balances.

Now, let us imagine that when the punt nua opens for trading
on Monday it falls 30 per cent and that NIR£1 trades at just €0.70.
The financial positions of Eddie and Tim, recalculated into euro,
would now look like those depicted in Table 5.3.

Table 5.3: Positions of Eddie and Tim with NIR£1 trading at €0.70

Monday	Fast Eddie	Thick Tim
Dublin	-€700,000	+€700,000
Belfast	+€1,000,000	-€1,000,000
Net position	+€300,000	-€300,000

In a matter of a few days, Fast Eddie's perfectly hedged position
has been transformed into a net position worth €300,000. Thick
Tim's position has gone in the opposite direction: his net position
is now worth minus €300,000. Eddie has made a huge profit, while
Tim has suffered a huge loss.

The Implications of Currency Redenomination

The implication of the illustrative example above is that people
will seek to protect their financial positions if a currency
redenomination and devaluation is feared. People will do this
by maximising their financial assets outside the State where
redenomination and devaluation is expected, and by maximising
their financial liabilities inside it. In this way they replicate the
direction of Fast Eddie's arrangements and they avoid the direction
followed by Thick Tim. But, if many people simultaneously seek to
maximise their deposits abroad while maximising their liabilities

at home, this could easily unleash a bank run, which would very quickly trigger a full-scale crisis.

The fear of triggering such a crisis is why public officials must always deny the possibility of a currency redenomination or currency devaluation until the very moment it happens. If public officials were to admit to even the remote possibility of a eurozone exit, they could trigger a cascade of events that would rapidly get out of control.

This is also why it is highly unlikely that any country would print new currency notes in advance of a eurozone exit. To print notes in a new currency 'on a precautionary basis' would be to admit the practical possibility of a eurozone exit. It would be very hard to keep such a development completely secret. News of it would probably leak and would likely raise doubts among depositors, thus triggering a destabilising bank run. This is why the possibility of eurozone exit will be officially denied even if it is being planned and even if it is fast approaching. Indeed, it will be denied *especially* if it is being planned and is fast approaching. Sir Henry Wotton, the English author, politician and diplomat, famously quipped that 'a diplomat is an honest man sent abroad to lie for his country.' We could rephrase the quip to state that a central banker is an honest man who must sometimes lie to his fellow countrymen for the sake of his country. This is the background to the first step of our detailed eurozone exit plan.

Ireland's Eurozone Exit Plan

Step 1 – Establish a Secret Government Working Group to Plan Eurozone Exit

A secret government working group comprising senior officials from key government ministries and the Central Bank should plan the key details of eurozone exit: drafting of announcements and laws, introduction of capital controls, declaration of a bank holiday to buy some extra time, redenomination of financial positions within the State, communications strategy with the public and the banks, and diplomatic strategy with EU partners.

Such a secret committee probably exists already today. In his most recent book, Pat Leahy reported that in the early months of the current Fine Gael–Labour government in 2011,

> [A] top-secret committee of senior officials from the departments of the Taoiseach, Finance, Public Expenditure and Justice, with others seconded in at various stages, was formed. . . . The committee began to work on a plan for what to do to ensure the functioning of the State and society in the event of a sudden Eurozone breakup, though some of its plan could equally have been utilized in the event of a default.[24]

Having established a working group to plan for the civil consequences of a default or eurozone break-up, it is unlikely that the Irish government is not also considering the economic, legal and diplomatic consequences.

Step 2 – Have the Oireachtas Create a New Currency on a Saturday
The announcement of eurozone exit and debt default could be made immediately. The simplest way to create a new currency would be to revert to Ireland's pre-euro currency and to establish the punt nua. All money, deposits and debts within the borders of the country would be redenominated into the new currency. To simplify this process, this should be done on a 1:1 basis, i.e. €1 = NIR£1. All euro-denominated debts or deposits held within the State's borders would be subject to the law passed by the Oireachtas and would be redenominated into punt nuas. Debts or deposits held outside the State would not be subject to the law.

But a formal and legally robust changeover of Ireland's legal tender would almost certainly require legislative underpinning. That would require the Oireachtas to vote on and pass legislation enacting the government's detailed plan. Weekends have long been the favoured time of the week for drastic shifts in governments' economic and financial policies. This is because banks are generally shut and there is a short time window for governments to act without fear of causing queues of anxious depositors outside the banks.

At the 2012 annual conference of the Irish Association of Corporate Treasurers, the Senior Cash and Debt Manager of building materials group CRH plc, Phil Shepherd said that his company did not leave cash in a eurozone bank over weekends. Instead, it used banks in Britain, the US and Asia.[25] The implication of the comments made by Shepherd was that CRH was concerned that, by depositing monies in the eurozone over weekends, it would make itself vulnerable to adverse weekend decisions made by eurozone finance ministers. This became the bitter experience of depositors in Cypriot banks in March 2013. As part of a deal to grant Cyprus a Troika bailout, one-off bank deposit levies of 6.7 per cent for deposits up to €100,000 and 9.9 per cent for higher deposits were announced for all domestic bank accounts. In theory, savers were compensated with shares in their banks. In practice, they suffered heavy losses.

Step 3 – Declare a Public Bank Holiday
It is often overlooked that a week-long bank holiday was successfully used in March 1933 by President Franklin Roosevelt as part of his policy to stem a damaging month-long run on US banks.[26] A bank holiday lasting one day to one week would buy the authorities additional time to manage the creation of and changeover to the new currency. It would allow banks to stamp all their notes, prevent withdrawals of euro and make any necessary changes to their electronic payment systems.

Step 4 – Impose Capital Controls but Allow New Currency to Float Freely
It would rapidly become clear that a currency redenomination was underway and that this would, most likely, be followed by a sizeable currency devaluation. People would attempt to physically and electronically transfer their euros out of Ireland and into a jurisdiction where they would be free from devaluation risk. Capital controls and a speedy reorganisation of banks' electronic payment systems would be required to prevent old euros from leaving the country and being deposited elsewhere.

At the same time, the new currency would be allowed to trade freely once international currency markets reopened. The resulting devaluation would contribute significantly to restoring lost competitiveness for those sectors that generate foreign revenue, such as manufacturing, agriculture, tourism and international services. The resulting competitiveness boost would act as a strong economic stimulus.

In time, i.e. after at least six months and after Ireland has had a very considerable competitiveness boost, consideration could be given to eventually re-associating the punt with sterling. That association between punt and sterling worked from 1922 to 1979 without substantial troubles. Ireland and Britain together enjoy many of the conditions required for an effective monetary union. So there is an obvious solution to Ireland's currency question lying at our doorstep, if it were judged that Ireland was too small to sustain an independent currency in the long term. But, if a small country like Iceland can maintain its own currency, why couldn't Ireland?

Step 5 – Stamp Old Notes and Print Notes

It would be a number of weeks before sufficient punt nuas could be printed. And, whatever about the large proportion of transactions now conducted via electronic banking, we would still need notes before newly printed paper notes would be available.

The existing physical infrastructure of the euro notes already circulating within the State would be used for this purpose. Existing euro notes would be stamped with ink or with physical stamps to make clear that these notes were now punt nuas (and therefore no longer euros). This would permit the old notes to circulate within the State as punt nuas, while preventing them from being exported from the State to be deposited elsewhere as euros. Meanwhile, the task of printing new notes could commence in earnest now that Plan B was out in the open. Once enough new notes were printed, they would be exchanged for the old stamped notes, and the latter would cease to be legal tender and would be retired from circulation.

Step 6 – Redefine the Mandate and Powers of the Central Bank

The focus and functions of the Irish Central Bank would change fundamentally upon the country's departure from the eurozone. It should be charged, as it was before the introduction of the euro, with responsibility for all monetary policy, payment systems and reserve management. And it should remember that countries exiting currency zones that have adopted prudent monetary policies have enjoyed rapidly falling inflation and strong economic growth, while countries that have used their central banks to print money have experienced instead hyperinflation and large economic contractions. The Central Bank should therefore be mandated with maintaining a low inflation target. In order to minimise the danger of hyperinflation or high inflation, the Central Bank should retain its institutional independence and be prohibited by law from directly monetising fiscal liabilities, i.e. from printing money to finance government spending deficits.

In order to counteract the deflationary impact of bankruptcies and insolvencies – triggered by many households and corporations inadvertently having a similar financial structure to that of Thick Tim – the Central Bank should supply a very large amount of liquidity to its own banking system against good collateral. The government should also recapitalise Ireland's banks.

It is likely that the Irish economy would experience significant inflationary impulses following eurozone exit, as a result of significant devaluation driving the costs of imported goods sharply upwards and the Central Bank providing generous liquidity in the immediate wake of that exit. But there would still be significant deflationary pressures as a legacy of Ireland's property bust and fragile banking system. So it should be possible for the Irish Central Bank to contain inflation once the initial devaluation effect had subsided. That was certainly the experience of Iceland. Iceland's currency devalued in 2008 by over 50 per cent because of its banking and financial crisis. As a result, inflation in Iceland approached 20 per cent in 2009.[27] But this was brought down below 5 per cent in 2011.

Step 7 – Notify Foreign Authorities so They Can Limit Any Contagion
If Ireland exited the euro, it would put added pressure on those remaining eurozone members that already have doubts over their continued membership of the single currency zone. Within those countries, the immediate temptation facing any local Fast Eddies

would be to take their deposits out of local banks and to redeposit them outside national territory where they would be free from redenomination and devaluation risk. An Irish eurozone exit would therefore put very considerable pressure on the commercial banks of members of the eurozone periphery. If depositors withdrew funds in considerable amounts, those banks might face acute short-term funding problems.

If Ireland sought a restructuring of its debts and – pending resolution of the matter – immediately started to default on government debt obligations as they fell due, many commercial banks in the eurozone core would face considerable financial pressure. Such banks would be left holding loan assets that were now defaulting and they would face losses on these loans. This could lead to a sharp reduction in depositor confidence in the solvency of affected banks. If depositors withdrew funds in considerable amounts, those banks, too, might face acute short-term funding problems.

In order to minimise the danger and extent of such financial contagion, once the Irish authorities have decided to opt for eurozone exit and debt restructuring they should immediately notify the ECB and other global central banks. This would enable those central banks to provide ample liquidity to their banks to counteract the inevitable stresses in the financial system and interbank lending markets that could result from the Irish authorities' decision.

Step 8 – Facilitate Expedited Bankruptcy Proceedings

Many individuals, corporations and banks have financing arrangements similar to those of Thick Tim: they have borrowed abroad to fund investments in Ireland. In international currency terms, the value of their Irish assets would be reduced through devaluation, while the value of their foreign liabilities would remain unchanged. That would lead to a reduction in the value of their balance sheet equity, which is simply a measure of total assets less total liabilities. For some, this would make the critical difference between having a financial situation that is fragile and one that is impossible. A eurozone exit, redenomination of financial assets and liabilities within the territory of the State, and a sharp currency devaluation are therefore likely to precipitate a fresh wave of bankruptcies and insolvencies.

The Irish authorities could respond in two ways to this development. They could either force these bankruptcies through the existing system, which would result in a lot of capable people putting their lives on hold for many years while they awaited the eventual outcome of this process. Alternatively, the authorities could change Ireland's legal framework to facilitate expedited bankruptcy proceedings. This would lead to some embarrassing injustices as a result of the curtailed legal scrutiny it would inevitably involve. But it would free up a lot of people to get on with the rest of their lives and to deploy their gifts in a productive, forward-looking way rather than in an unproductive battle about the past. Ireland should opt for the second approach, however vehement the protests of its lawyers and judges might be.

Step 9 – Begin Negotiations to Restructure Sovereign Debt
The Paris Club is an informal group of official creditors whose role is to find coordinated and sustainable solutions to the payment difficulties experienced by debtor countries.[28] The origin of the Paris Club dates back to 1956 when Argentina agreed to meet its public creditors in Paris. Since then, the Paris Club has reached 429 agreements with 90 different debtor countries. Since 1956, the debt treated within the framework of Paris Club agreements has amounted to $573 billion. On its website, the Paris Club identifies the benefits it brings to both debtors and creditors:

> *For creditors, the Club is an efficient and coordinated forum for the recovery of claims and acts as a leveraging force through its longstanding expertise in terms of debt restructuring and debt collection. A coordinated creditor voice also helps to promote respect for debtors' payment obligations in the long run.*
>
> *For debtors, avoiding protracted periods of default and arrears helps promote access to new lending from private and official sources and contributes to achieving the ultimate goal of sustainable economic development.[29]*

Ireland is already a member of this group. It should now use that position to seek an agreed restructuring of its own debts.

Step 10 – Begin Negotiations on Ireland's Debts Owed to the ECB
Ireland – through its Central Bank – owed the ECB nearly €60 billion as of September 2013.[30] The simplest solution for Ireland would be to simply renege on these debts. After all, the ECB is the institution that has played the central role in driving the Irish economy to the edge of destruction. If there was ever justice in applying the 'You break it; you pay for it' rule, it would be in the case of the debts owed by the Irish Central Bank to the ECB.

Nonetheless, we are members of the EU and we wish to conduct our affairs in a responsible way. Ireland should therefore open negotiations with the ECB on the State's liabilities to it. But our opening negotiating position should be that we owe these people nothing.

WINNERS AND LOSERS
There would be several clear winners and losers in the event of an Irish eurozone exit and debt default (see Table 5.4).

Table 5.4: Likely Winners and Losers in the Event of a Eurozone Exit and Debt Default

Likely Winners	Likely Losers
Fast Eddie: those who borrowed in Ireland to invest abroad	Thick Tim: those who borrowed abroad to invest at home
Manufacturers and those working in agriculture	Bankers
Borrowers	Depositors
Exporters	Importers
Domestic tourism sector	Package holiday companies
Young workers	Welfare recipients
Those governing in 2–3 years	Those governing now
	Lenders to the Irish government, including the EU, ECB and IMF (Troika)

Fast Eddie and Thick Tim

The clearest winners in an Irish eurozone exit would be those, like Fast Eddie, who had borrowed in Ireland to invest abroad. With the devaluation of the punt nua, their borrowings would be devalued while their (foreign) assets would retain their full value. They would profit handsomely from the move.

The clearest losers would be those, like Thick Tim, who had done the opposite and borrowed abroad to invest in Ireland. They could lose heavily in the move. Many Irish households and companies could inadvertently find themselves in this position. Their continuing solvency could be fundamentally called into question by the development, i.e. following the change, their assets might no longer exceed their liabilities and they may have negative equity. Thus, they may find it difficult to pay their financial liabilities as they fall due.

Many foreign multinationals could also find themselves sharing ranks with Thick Tim. For they often use loans from parent companies based abroad to finance investments in factories and plants here in Ireland. But, while many foreign multinationals would suffer from this effect, they would also profit handsomely from their status as manufacturers.

Manufacturers, Those Working in Agriculture and Bankers

Multinational manufacturers would, in general, be clear winners in the event of an Irish eurozone exit. Their revenue is mostly generated outside the State and would retain its dollar value. At the same time, many of their costs occur within the State, and these would be devalued and would thus drop in dollar terms. This would lead to a boost in the operating profitability of multinationals in Ireland that could be quite significant. It could increase the prospects of additional multinational investment and jobs creation in Ireland.

So, while multinational manufacturers may see a deterioration in the balance sheet value of their equity – as a result of the Thick Tim effect – they would also see an improvement in their operating profitability. In the longer term, the senior management in multinationals are more likely to be enthused by the increase in the underlying operating profitability of their Irish units than they would be concerned about their once-off balance sheet deterioration.

Agriculture would benefit from a eurozone exit, as it is an exporting industry that sells its goods at prices set internationally while facing costs that are largely set domestically.

Bankers would, on the other hand, be clear losers in an Irish eurozone exit. For, in a key respect, their financing structure resembles that of Thick Tim. A substantial portion of the funding of the Irish banking system is borrowed abroad, while the bulk of its monies are lent within the State. The international currency value of the banks' assets would drop, while the value of a significant portion of their funding – the foreign element – would remain unchanged. This would lead to a drop in the value of the banks' equity (i.e. total assets less total liabilities) and the renewed threat of bankruptcy. As of September 2013, Irish-based banks were borrowing a total of €264 billion from foreign lenders.[31] In addition to partially suffering from the Thick Tim effect, banks would also lose out as a result of being large investors in Irish government bonds. With the Irish government seeking a restructuring of, or a reduction in, the value of the debts it owes, those who own Irish government debt instruments (i.e. bonds) would face an immediate reduction in the value of their investments. This would put further downward pressure on the banks' equity and would further increase their prospects of renewed insolvency.

When the EU heads of government resolved in June 2012 that it was 'imperative to break the vicious circle between banks and sovereigns', they didn't really mean it.[32] What they did mean was that they wanted to reduce the danger of the failure of bank finances causing knock-on problems for public finances. If the cost to the public finances of Ireland's rescue of its banks was replicated across the eurozone periphery, it would drive the already fragile state finances of several countries over the edge and into insolvency. So it was logical for EU policy-makers to try and stem the tide of financial red ink spilling from commercial banks to sovereign states. But since that important EU summit in 2012, the financial links between banks and sovereigns have grown in one very important way.

Since 2011, commercial banks have bought substantial additional portions of sovereign (or government) debt. This has had the effect of increasing the price of government debt and reducing the implied interest rate on that debt. These developments have been pleasing to governments and to policy-makers because they demonstrate increasing financial stability within the eurozone. But they have come at the price of increasing the financial interdependence of banks and sovereigns. One academic paper has described this process as 'supportive of moral hazard':

> *Over time, there is an increase in 'home bias' – greater exposure of domestic banks to its sovereign's bonds – which is partly explained by the European Central Bank funding of these positions. On balance, our results are supportive of moral hazard in the form of risk-taking by under-capitalized banks to exploit low risk weights and central-bank funding of risky government bond positions.*[33]

If a sovereign was now to fail and to seek a restructuring of its debts, 'the vicious circle' would return. But this time, instead of financially failing banks putting fragile sovereign finances under pressure, the situation would be reversed. Financially failing sovereigns would now put fragile bank finances under pressure.

Borrowers and Depositors

Domestic borrowers would benefit from Ireland's exit from the eurozone, as the real – international currency – value of their borrowings would be devalued. Depositors would lose out as the real value of their deposits would drop.

Exporters and Importers

Exporters would benefit as, in domestic currency terms, their Irish costs would remain unchanged while the value of their export revenues would increase. Importers would face the opposite effect: the domestic currency cost of imports would rise steeply. So, for example, the cost of new cars would rise and, as a result, so too would the value of second-hand cars.

Domestic Tourism and Foreign Holiday Operators

Domestic tourism would benefit as Ireland would become a cheaper destination for foreign visitors. Foreign holiday operators would lose out as the holidays they offer would, at a stroke, become more expensive. Some Irish people, who might previously have holidayed abroad, would now find holidaying at home a more attractive economic proposition.

Young Workers and Welfare Recipients

As the Irish economy experienced a competitive stimulus as a result of currency devaluation and a reduction in its debt burden, there should be a return to strong economic growth and an increase in the pace of job creation. This would benefit young entrants to the workforce, who now often go abroad to find work.

But welfare recipients – including retirees – would probably be losers from the whole process. With imported goods becoming more expensive as a result of Ireland's currency devaluation, their regular receipts would be worth less in real terms.

Those Governing in the Future and Those Governing Now

Those governing at the time of Ireland's exit from the euro would be likely to suffer the brunt of mounting fear and anger. Such emotions would probably mount quickly, with banks closing for several days, questions being raised over the continuity of supply of some key imports and a growing realisation (for many of those sharing Thick Tim's financial predicament) of the implications of Ireland's currency devaluation. It is unlikely that many citizens would blame themselves for failing to foresee this calamity. It is far more likely that they would blame the government of the day. If the loss of political support suffered by Fianna Fáil between 2007 and 2011 is anything to go by, the presiding government parties could rapidly lose a lot of support.

But within 18 to 24 months, memories of the immediate shock should have dissipated, and the longer-term benefits of Ireland's competitive currency devaluation and freeing itself from the shackles of unbearable debt should start to bear visible fruit in terms of rising economic growth, employment and optimism. The political parties governing at this stage of the process may, as a result, harvest significant gains in popularity.

However, high and definite upfront costs with hard-to-quantify medium-term benefits would make exiting the eurozone a neuralgic option for politicians. But the political calculus may be different for a new government at the start of its term of office. It might knowingly incur the upfront cost of eurozone exit at the start of its term, expecting that, as its term advanced, voters would eventually see the benefits of its decision. As the next general election approached, this government might reasonably expect to be surfing a wave of popularity for having finally sorted out Ireland's economic crisis.

Lenders to the Irish Government, Including the Troika

Obvious losers in a process that would see the government freeing itself from a substantial part of its debt burden would be those who have lent to the Irish government. The losers would include those who had bought government debt (i.e. government bonds) in the open market, including banks, and pension and investment funds. Losers may also include the Irish government's official creditors: the EU and the IMF have lent substantial monies to the Irish government, while the ECB has lent substantial amounts to the Irish Central Bank. Ireland's debts would now become the subject of negotiation and possible legal dispute.

ARGUMENTS AGAINST PLAN B

Having Endured this Far, Now is Not the Time to Give Up

The Argument

Ireland has already endured approximately €30 billion of difficult budgetary adjustments, the Troika has just departed and an end to austerity is in sight, according to those who should know. In December 2012, Tánaiste Eamon Gilmore stated that the previous month's budget meant that an end to crippling tax hikes and tough spending cuts was nearly in sight. And, in July 2013, Minister for

Finance Michael Noonan told a meeting, 'We have a difficult budget coming up in October.... However, once delivered, we will be within touching distance of the 3 per cent deficit target and the days of massive budget adjustments will be behind us.'[34] So, it could be argued, now is not the time to succumb to Plan B when Plan A is already bearing fruit and an end to austerity is near.

The Answer

There are several reasons why this thinking is wrong. First, Plan A is not working. The main symptom of the eurozone economic crisis is alarmingly high debt levels. But Plan A is not succeeding in reducing them. Aggregate debt levels, comprising public sector, corporate and household debt, continue to rise relative to GDP across the eurozone periphery.

Second, as detailed in Chapter 4, budgetary austerity is not over. In his July 2013 comments, the Minister for Finance was referring to the requirement that EU member states should not borrow more than 3 per cent of their annual output. However, under the Fiscal Compact, which we signed up to in 2012, the EU also requires countries to reduce their structural (or underlying) deficit to just 0.5 per cent of GDP. And they require countries to reduce their national debt to just 60 per cent of GDP over 20 years. Our national debt is currently running at twice that level.

Having reduced our annual borrowing to just 3 per cent of GDP, Ireland will have to further reduce that figure to just 0.5 per cent of GDP. That means a further 2.5 per cent of deficit reduction will be required. And, given the counter-productive and deflationary impact which such measures initially generate, budgetary reduction measures totalling around 5 per cent of GDP are probably required. This all means that, even after the stiff measures still to come in Budget 2015, further austerity measures – spending cuts and tax increases – of over €8 billion may still be needed.

Third, enormous economic problems remain in the private sector. The finances of Ireland's banks remain fragile at best. Company and household indebtedness levels remain as mortgage arrears continue to mount. Domestic demand has shown little sign of growth since 2008. So even if the problems of the public finances were fixed – and they haven't been – massive private sector problems would remain.

Fourth, even if all of the economic imbalances that have been unleashed by the eurozone could be reversed by magic, it would be inevitable that the flaws of the common currency would generate fresh economic imbalances. Ireland had no serious economic imbalances in the mid-1990s when it committed to joining the new currency. But a decade of interest rates that were inappropriately low for Ireland spawned credit, construction and cost bubbles. This central flaw – inappropriate national interest rates – remains at the heart of the euro and is the fundamental reason why Ireland should never have joined the common currency.

The EU Has Helped Us Already, and It Will Help Us Again

The Argument
Why should we walk away from the euro (and from Europe) when the EU has already done so much for Ireland and would be willing to help us again?

The Answer
Europe has helped us enormously before. And it would be a regret of the first order for Ireland to have to leave the euro. But it is an illusion to believe that Europe has the financial capacity or the political will to do what is required to save the entire eurozone periphery, i.e. to go for a full fiscal and political union or donate hundreds of billions of euros to the distressed periphery.

At every stage of the crisis, the core countries of the eurozone have done just enough to prevent the problems of the periphery from spilling over to become problems of the core. So they have given Ireland emergency loans, to stop Ireland and its banks defaulting on loans owed to banks in the core; they have given us interest rate reductions and debt maturity extensions, to maintain the appearance that Ireland is solvent and that the core will be repaid its loans. But they have never given us enough help to solve the crisis. This is largely because the sums involved (if Spain and Italy also required help) are simply beyond the political and economic capacity of the core countries of the eurozone. So the members of the eurozone periphery resemble victims whose ship has sunk and who are treading water in rough seas. The ship of the eurozone core has drawn up alongside. And it has thrown out ropes for the victims to hold onto. This is sufficient to prevent any of them from drowning. But the captain of the eurozone core refuses to allow any of the hapless victims on board his ship: enough will be done to prevent anyone drowning and to prevent the crisis getting worse, but not enough will be done to truly end the crisis.

Ireland is Solemnly Committed to Ever-Closer EU Union

The Argument
In European treaties, Ireland has committed itself to forge an 'ever-closer union' with the other countries of the EU. Abandoning the euro would represent a big step in the opposite direction and would be a breach of a solemn undertaking.

The Answer
Treaties are no more than expressions of political will, which can, in extreme circumstances, be abandoned. The 1800 Act of Union, for example, committed Britain and Ireland to 'for ever after, be united into one kingdom'. But, by 1920, it was clear to all that this commitment would have to be abandoned. And it was.

The euro project is fast approaching the point when it will be recognised that the costs of holding it together exceed its benefits. In pursuing Plan A we have fought the good fight. But there's no point in us fighting a battle that's going to destroy us.

Legal Doubts

The Argument
There is no legal or treaty basis for a country to unilaterally exit the euro. For Ireland to exit the euro would be a fundamental breach of legal commitments solemnly entered into.

The Answer

It was Cicero who stated that 'Salus populi suprema lex esto' ('The well-being of the people should be the supreme law'). French President Charles de Gaulle put it more earthily when he said, 'Treaties are like maidens and roses: they each have their day.'[35] An ECB legal working paper admits as much when it states: 'There are three hypothetical circumstances where a Member State could, in extreme circumstances, assert a right of unilateral withdrawal.'[36] The third circumstance listed in the document was, 'a Member State faces extraordinary difficulties that prevent it complying with its treaty obligations.'[37] Ireland is now at that point.

With youth unemployment rates in excess of 50 per cent, with reports of people deliberately injecting themselves with the HIV virus in order to qualify for public health care and with the worrying rise in popularity of a neo-Nazi political party, Greece has already gone far beyond it.

Inflation Risk

The Argument

If Ireland exited the euro, returned to the punt and allowed it to devalue significantly (e.g. by 30 per cent), then import costs would rise significantly, unleashing an inflationary spiral.

The Answer

Ireland is suffering from such strong forces of deflation – aftershocks of property bust, construction sector stagnation and government austerity policies – that even the inflationary effect of a currency devaluation is unlikely to trigger significant inflation. That has been the recent experience of both Britain and Iceland. They are both suffering from strong deflationary impulses and, over the last five years, have had 30 per cent and 50 per cent currency devaluations respectively. But, after an initial rise, inflation in each country remains subdued.

Contagion Worry

The Argument

An Irish eurozone exit and unilateral debt restructuring would probably be accompanied by other countries doing the same. For these countries to gain a reduction in their liabilities, other entities must suffer a loss in their assets. That could trigger the same sort of financial contagion that was unleashed when Lehman Brothers went bust in September 2008. Even before that financial disaster, British Prime Minister Gordon Brown warned a close aide:

> *Do you realise how bad this is going to get? We're going to be in recession by the New Year. And there's nothing we can do. And people will make that the big issue, but that's not the worst of it. The whole bloody thing could collapse. I'm serious. The whole bloody thing.*[38]

As US Secretary of the Treasury Tim Geithner said in September 2011, European policy-makers must avoid the 'threat of cascading default, bank runs and catastrophic risk'.[39]

The Answer

First, in considering whether and to what extent they should offer financial help to Ireland, other countries must consider their national interests. In considering whether to remain within or to exit the eurozone, Ireland must consider its own national interests. We should not assume enormous financial responsibilities so that others may escape theirs. But we should nonetheless alert the ECB and other central banks of our plans in advance, so that they may provide whatever emergency liquidity that would be required for their own banking systems, if they fear financial contagion.

Second, the eurozone crisis has been bubbling away for several years now. Most large banks and corporations have already made arrangements to limit the impact on them of any eurozone fragmentation. The simplest way for them to limit such impact is to match assets and liabilities in the countries that might exit, thus generating a natural hedge in the event of eurozone fragmentation.

So if a foreign multinational has large Irish assets, for example, an investment in a large factory with expensive equipment, a natural hedge can be achieved by funding those Irish assets with Irish borrowings. That way, if Irish assets and liabilities were redenominated from euros into punt nuas, and if the punt nua subsequently dropped sharply in value, the fall in value of the multinational's assets would be largely offset by the fall in value of its funding liabilities, and any net loss would thus be minimised.

This is one important reason behind the large rise in Target 2 balances over recent years. These balances record loans between national central banks within the eurozone. As foreign multinationals extract funds to head office and require local branches to replace them with local funding, there has been a flow of monies out of the periphery and back into the centre of the eurozone. To compensate for this, periphery central banks have had to borrow large funds from core central banks via Target 2 balances. In September 2013, the Irish Central Bank owed the system €53 billion, while the Bundesbank was owed €570 billion.[40] The bottom line is that a lot of banks and multinational corporations have already arranged their finances to withstand the effects of eurozone fragmentation.

Third, there are concrete steps that can be taken to calm international markets. Central banks should use all the available tools at their disposal to prevent liquidity crises from becoming solvency crises. As the international research service Variant Perception has pointed out:

Central banks and governments should: recapitalise banks, provide greater disclosure on solvency and liquidity of banks, expand the eligible collateral in order to reduce any collateral squeeze, provide high quality assets for repurchase agreements (a means by which banks turn illiquid collateral into cash), allow non-bank companies to participate in repurchase facilities, and provide sovereign interbank lending guarantees.[41]

Currency Redenomination and Devaluation Could Kill the IFSC

The Argument
A lot of the business done by banks in Dublin's International
Financial Services Centre (IFSC) involves hedging foreign currency
risks for customers operating internationally. To arbitrarily require
entities operating within a commercial enclave such as the IFSC to
redenominate their euro positions into punt nua positions, which
would then devalue, would cause so much chaos that it could risk
killing off the IFSC and the 32,700 well-paid jobs there.[42]

The Answer
As an exceptional case, financial institutions operating within the
IFSC could be exempt from the requirement to redenominate euro
positions into punt nua positions.

Plan B Would Render Our Banks Insolvent Once More

The Argument
The solvency of Ireland's banks would be threatened at several
levels by Plan B. The banks own substantial holdings of Irish
government bonds. A default by the Irish government on its debts
would cause financial losses on those holdings. The banks are owed
money by many individuals and companies that would be pushed
into insolvency by currency redenomination and devaluation,
which would threaten the banks' own solvency. Finally, the banks'
own financing arrangements resemble those of Thick Tim in one
key respect: they borrow monies abroad on interbank markets,
which are invested or lent at home. So the banks would be major
losers under a currency redenomination and devaluation. Having
pumped billions into rescuing the banks, must Ireland's citizens
see them go bust once again?

The Answer
It is true. Ireland's banks would probably be rendered insolvent
once again by Plan B. But they may be structurally insolvent anyway.
Plan B may merely crystallise losses that are already baked in the

cake, so to speak. For Ireland's banks cannot prosper if Ireland faces many years of stagnation and economic disappointment.

The key point is that any government planning for a debt default and eurozone exit would also have to plan to recapitalise or reconstitute Ireland's banks. Scarce government funds would have to be shepherded into Ireland's banks after D-Day and after Ireland executes Plan B. In addition, emergency liquidity funding from Ireland's Central Bank would have to be made available. But, by the end of this process, Ireland would still have a functioning banking system. The key difference is that that system would then face an economy that is growing rather than stagnating.

The Troika Is More Trusted to Run Things than National Authorities

The Argument
Ireland gets into severe economic difficulties every 25 years or so as result of calamitous policy errors. Protectionism in the 1950s led to dismal economic growth and emigration on a vast scale. Fiscal profligacy in the late 1970s and early 1980s led to the very same results. Since 2007 Ireland has had to grapple with another economic disaster that is leading, yet again, to the same results. The problem isn't with Europe. It lies with short-sighted Irish voters and politicians. A debt restructuring and eurozone exit would put the economic fate of the country back in the hands of the same Irish policy elite that has repeatedly made a dog's dinner of things in the past. Give me rule from Europe any day in preference to local incompetence.

The Answer
It is true that Ireland has made grave economic policy errors in the past. But Ireland and its voters have learned hard lessons from these bitter experiences. The protectionism of the 1950s was replaced by the opening up of our economy, which has massively boosted living standards and brought major multinationals (and jobs) to Ireland. The fiscal incontinence of the late 1970s and early 1980s was followed by a sustained political consensus of 'never again'.

Ireland's current crisis is, as this book attempts to explain, fundamentally different in nature to earlier crises. But Ireland's policy-makers have tended to see this crisis in terms of the public finance crisis of the 1980s, during which they grew to political maturity. And they have reacted to this current crisis according to how they think the earlier crisis should have been combatted. So Brian Cowen and Brian Lenihan pushed through severe budgetary adjustments in a patriotic spirit, even though they knew those measures would cause them immense political damage. The same can said for Enda Kenny and Eamon Gilmore. In my view, policy-makers have generally reacted with honour and patriotism to this crisis, even if they have been profoundly misguided.

It is the key contention of this book that there has been a failure by Official Ireland to accurately diagnose this crisis. The roots of the crisis lie in Europe and not in Ireland. But, while Ireland is a small country with a clear political culture that can record and learn from its mistakes, Europe is a big, amorphous political entity with no clear political culture, no clear political accountability and, as yet, no clear capacity to learn from its mistakes. So, even though there would be major challenges facing Irish institutions as they adapted to a new life outside the eurozone, I would rather take my chances with my friends, my neighbours and my country than stick with a Europe that is run by technocrats, fearful of democracy and resentful of its own people.

Exit Costs Would Be Huge – The Cure Would Kill the Patient

The Argument
The immediate costs of eurozone exit would be huge. As mentioned, Ireland's banks would probably be rendered insolvent all over again. A currency changeover would have to be managed under conditions of acute economic stress and uncertainty. Capital controls would have to be rapidly installed. The reaction of the EU would be uncertain: at best, they would seek to cooperate and to work through the resulting problems with us; at worst, a trade war could result.

The Answer

The costs of eurozone exit would not be principally caused by that exit; rather, exiting the eurozone would force a recognition of costs that already exist. Despite pretending that all is well, Ireland's banks are arguably already insolvent.

Currency unions have broken up elsewhere at short notice without necessarily having damaging long-term effects. The EU is unlikely to want to compound the damage of eurozone fragmentation with a trade war at a time when global financial markets are already showing considerable fragility.

06 EPILOGUE

*We have no eternal allies and we have
no perpetual enemies. Our interests are
eternal and perpetual, and those interests
it is our duty to follow.*

Lord Palmerston

EASTERN GERMANY 1991

In March 1991 I went to work in Weißenfels in Eastern Germany as Financial Controller of a large industrial bakery. One hour's drive from the city of Leipzig, Weißenfels had been part of the German Democratic Republic just eighteen months earlier. But, after German reunification in October 1990, it was now part of the Federal Republic.

I arrived at a time of enormous economic upheaval and change. The East Germans not only had to cope with the consequences of changing from a communist, command economy to a mixed, social market economy but they also had to deal with the consequences of monetary union with their West German cousins. The big problem was that, while monetary union took place on terms that imparted a large short-term boost, those terms also had economically calamitous longer-term consequences. The central problem facing German policy-makers as they contemplated German monetary reunification was what the exchange rate should be between the western Deutschmark and the soon-to-be-phased-out Ostmark. Obviously it would have suited those East Germans with large Ostmark savings to have as high a conversion rate as possible so that they might end up with as many Deutschmarks as possible. But setting the exchange rate too high would make East German labour too expensive and would lead to high unemployment. The estimated market rate at the time was 4.3 Ostmarks for every Deutschmark (4.3:1).[1]

West Germany's political leadership under Chancellor Helmut Kohl had several reasons for setting an exchange rate that would put a higher value on the Ostmark. It would have been easier to suggest that German reunification was a unity of equals with an exchange rate of parity (1:1). Older East Germans, with substantial Ostmark savings and with Ostmark pension entitlements, would have been major beneficiaries of a low exchange rate. And setting a low exchange rate would have avoided a feared flood of internal migration. If the rate was set at a high rate, say 4.3:1, this would have meant that wage rates in East Germany would have been only a small fraction of those in West Germany. This would have inevitably led to a destabilising flood of internal migration as East Germans abandoned low-paying jobs in search of higher-paying jobs in West Germany.

On the other hand, there were compelling reasons not to set the exchange rate at parity. Even at the market exchange rate of 4.3:1, East German businesses were not competitive in world markets. Slashing that rate to parity would have, at one stroke, made nearly every East German business structurally insolvent. Goods that previously had an international cost of 1 Deutschmark would have now cost 4.3 Deutschmarks. A bad cost competitiveness situation would have been transformed into a calamitous one. And, instead of pay differences driving huge internal German migration, it would have been driven by high unemployment levels.

That is why, in an attempt to balance up the arguments, the West German monetary authorities in the Bundesbank recommended an exchange rate of 2:1.[2] In this way, they thought, it might prove possible to balance the threats of having an exchange rate that was too low and one that was too high. However, the decision was taken out of their hands when Chancellor Kohl and his government decided on an exchange rate of 1:1. This decision was immensely popular in Eastern Germany and contributed significantly to the surprisingly strong showing of Kohl's CDU/CSU party in Germany's 1990 general election.

But, while East Germans could celebrate the fact that their savings were converted straight into Deutschmarks, it was only with the passage of time that the damaging effect of the conversion rate on the competitiveness of East German industry became clear. For real wages in East Germany were, at one stroke, elevated to West German levels. But, after half a century of economic mismanagement under communist rule, East German productivity levels lagged far behind those in West Germany. The result was inevitable: the insolvency and closure of most of East Germany's industry, the lay-off of most industrial workers and massive migration of people from East to West Germany as they searched for work.

While the outside world may look at German reunification and consider it an economic success, the hard facts suggest otherwise. Today, the figures suggest that GDP per capita in the former East Germany is roughly 70 per cent of that in the western regions, and the unemployment rate in the former East Germany exceeds 12 per cent, which is more than twice that in the west of the country.

Between 1990 and 2007, the population of Weiβenfels fell from 37,765 to just 29,569, a drop of over 20 per cent. Over the same period, the population of German Chancellor Angela Merkel's home town of Templin, also in the former East Germany, has fallen by 15 per cent.

When I left Weiβenfels in 1993 there were only three industrial units of any size still operating: the bakery where I worked, which had to be near its customers if products were to arrive fresh; and the creamery and the bacon factory, each of which had to be close to the farms from where product was sourced. Weiβenfels, which had once been the 'Shoe Metropolis of the German Democratic Republic', had no notable shoe production left. The shoe factories had been driven out of business by overly high costs resulting from an exchange rate that was too high.

EAST GERMANY: THE LESSONS FOR IRELAND
The economic experience of East Germany provides two warnings to Ireland. First, real effective exchange rates (REER) matter enormously even if they are not very well understood. For they

represent the price of an area's goods and services abroad. If your REER is too high, as was the case with East Germany, you risk pricing yourself out of markets, and a slow-motion economic depression and the widespread departure of young and talented people can result. This process can last several decades.

The second lesson for Ireland is that even full fiscal union – where an area's debts are taken over and its welfare bills are underwritten – is a very poor substitute for the fundamental misalignment of costs that an overly high REER represents. The populations of East Germany's neighbours, Poland, the Czech Republic and Slovakia, have not suffered anything like the implosion witnessed in East Germany. Sure, those countries didn't have the economic sugar daddy of the Federal Republic of Germany. So their initial adjustment to the hard economic realities of competitive markets in the 1990s was much more difficult. But, unlike East Germany, those countries retained their national currencies and those currencies operated at levels that allowed for the survival of large tracts of their indigenous industry. From an economic perspective, it can be strongly argued that Poland, the Czech Republic and Slovakia have done better following the fall of the Berlin Wall than the former East Germany.

Euro enthusiasts suggest that the answer to our problems would be European political and fiscal union. It is argued that the problem with European Monetary Union is that it doesn't go far enough. Without the regular cash transfers represented by a fiscal union and a common system of banking regulation, it is asserted that EMU is incomplete. But it is a complete fallacy to believe that European political and fiscal union would represent anything other than an additional made-in-Europe calamity for Ireland. The experience of East Germany points clearly in that direction. And that's before we consider the inevitable loss of national sovereignty that any such move would involve. As the centenary of the 1916 Easter Rising approaches, a greater rhetorical emphasis on tales of national derring-do and Irish sovereignty is being accompanied by the reality that ever-greater portions of national sovereignty are being handed over or lost.

IRELAND'S POLITICAL CHOICE

On 1 August 1800, the Irish Parliament approved the Act of Union (Ireland). This, and the earlier passage through the House of Commons of the Union with Ireland Act 1800, determined Ireland's constitutional status for over a century. Ireland was to be a mere constituent part of the United Kingdom of Great Britain and Ireland.

The Act of Union was pushed through by Britain in 1800 in the wake of the French Revolution (1789–1799) and the Irish Rebellion of 1798. The strength of that rebellion had profoundly unsettled Ireland's British rulers and it had been repressed with utter savagery. The subsequent Act of Union was, believe it or not, conceived as a political act of conciliation in the wake of that repression. It was argued that Irish Catholics would be better treated by Protestant rulers in London than by Protestant rulers in Dublin.

But when the proposal for the Act of Union was first put to the Irish Parliament it was rejected by a vote of 109 to 104. In a strategy that would be echoed over two centuries later with the ratification of the Lisbon Treaty, essentially the same question was asked a second time. The second vote in 1800 saw the Act of Union pass comfortably through the Irish Parliament by a vote of 158 to 115, a majority achieved in part through bribery. General Cornwallis allowed government rice to be sold in poorer parts of Dublin at low prices in order to save 'many from starvation'. Money from the secret service vote (£26 million in today's terms) and the plentiful award of peerages and honours to critics were used to sway the decision of the Irish Parliament.

Ireland resided unhappily within the United Kingdom in the century that followed. The promise of religious conciliation, which the Union had supposedly offered, was dashed when King George III vetoed Catholic emancipation. The indifference of their rulers to the needs of Irish peasants saw the Great Famine claim the lives of around one million of their number. Another million emigrated. The Land War, the rise and fall of Charles Stuart Parnell and the promise of Home Rule all followed. Eventually it was the armed rebellion of 1916, the historic general election vote of 1918 and the War of Independence which saw the Act of Union reversed.

Ireland may shortly be confronted with a similar choice to that which faced the country's parliamentarians in 1800: accept a significant and possibly terminal loss of sovereignty in return for immediate financial help and inducements. If Ireland cannot pay its own debts and if Europe cannot face the consequences of default by Ireland (and Greece and Portugal) then Europe will have to settle our bills for us.

However, Europe would require a political price for such a massive fiscal transfer. That price would involve a further large sacrifice of national independence along the lines suggested in 2011 by then President of the ECB Jean-Claude Trichet when he called for the establishment of an EU finance ministry. Of more importance to Ireland, Trichet went on to say that, while international bailouts of countries in exchange for their pledges to reform their finances were reasonable as an initial response to debt crises, 'if a country is still not delivering, I think all would agree that the second stage has to be different.'[3] He was suggesting that eurozone authorities should then be given 'a much deeper and authoritative say in the formation of the country's economic policies if these go harmfully astray'.[4]

IRELAND'S ECONOMIC CHOICE

Even if Europe doesn't force the political question of sacrificing sovereignty in return for financial help, Ireland still faces a heavy economic choice. On 1 October 2013, Dr Pippa Malmgren, economic advisor to former US President George W. Bush, said that Ireland faced 20 years of 'no growth' if we stayed within the eurozone because the ECB is unable to stoke inflation to help reduce our debt woes. She said that Ireland could deal with its debts through austerity without inflating them away:

> But you have to accept 20 years of no growth. That's the only other option. It's what European policymakers expect Ireland to do. The question is, do the Irish people have the tolerance to take that much pain?

She went on to say that a country – possibly Cyprus – will eventually leave the eurozone: 'If a country can leave and devalue, it raises the question for Ireland – what is the cost of staying in?'[5]

The choice facing the Irish people is simple and brutal: we can make further sacrifices of national sovereignty, remain inside the eurozone and condemn ourselves to inappropriate economic policies that will deny us noticeable economic growth for a long time. Or we can trigger enormous economic disruption in the short term, but with the longer-term view of restoring economic growth by being free from debts that are unsustainable and through currency devaluation.

THE FINAL DECISION WILL COME DOWN TO POLITICS

In the end, any decision by Ireland to abandon the euro and to restructure its debts will come down to politics. To begin with, a decision to exit the euro would reverse the political direction that Ireland has followed since Easter 1916: less Britain and more Europe. Furthermore, any decision to exit would bring on certain and large upfront costs in return for large but only probable benefits in the medium term. This is not the sort of decision for which politicians are renowned. However, a new government – with a fresh mandate and the political capacity to endure costs at the start of its term in return for benefits towards the end – might well find it attractive.

Whatever a government's political calculus concerning this question, it is highly unlikely that an Irish government would ever make it unilaterally. For all of our bravado and celebration of rebel acts, we lack the moral courage to turn around to the EU and say that its currency union is an emperor with no clothes. As a people, we often lack the moral courage to even say whether we would prefer a cup of tea or a cup of coffee. Our typical reaction is often, 'Ah sure, I wouldn't like to put you to any effort. What are you having yourself?'

An Irish eurozone exit is therefore only likely in the context of other members abandoning the common currency area. If Cyprus or Italy was to abandon the euro, financial markets would quickly put pressure on other countries along the eurozone periphery to make a decision: in or out? Ireland needs to be ready to take that opportunity. Back in 1993, the forerunner of the eurozone – the European Exchange Rate Mechanism – came under huge pressure. Britain had to pull sterling out on what became referred to as Black Wednesday. Once Britain left, the door was open for Ireland to let the punt fall. As the then Secretary of the Department of Finance Maurice Doyle described the decision:

> *Look there's a point at which courage turns into stupidity. And we fought the good fight. There's no point in us fighting a battle which is going to destroy us on another front.*[6]

If we reach that point again, we need to be ready to implement Plan B.

GLOSSARY

Balance sheet recession – this occurs when highly indebted people and/or companies suffer a large drop in the value of their assets. Their equity (i.e. the value of their assets less the value of their liabilities) may turn negative.

CSO – Central Statistics Office.

Directorate General for Economic and Financial Affairs (DG ECFIN) – this is the directorate of the EU Commission responsible for economic matters. Since 2010, the Commissioner responsible for this directorate has been Olli Rehn.

ECB – European Central Bank.

ERM – Exchange Rate Mechanism, the forerunner of the euro, which retained national currencies but sought to limit variation in their movements against one another.

ESM – European Stability Mechanism. This is an EU body that provides financial assistance programmes for eurozone states that are in financial difficulty. It has a maximum lending capacity of €500 billion.

EU – European Union.

External devaluation/revaluation – external devaluation occurs when deflationary pressures in an economy are accommodated by a fall in its external exchange rate. Domestic prices and wages can thus fall in international (i.e. external) terms without having to fall in domestic (i.e. internal) terms. This is advantageous as prices and incomes will not fall relative to domestic debts. External revaluation is where inflationary pressures in an economy are accommodated by a rise in its external exchange rate. External devaluation and revaluation stand in contrast to internal devaluation/revaluation (see below).

GDP – Gross domestic product, a measure of a country's annual economic output using a geographic concept of output. If output is produced in a country it is included in that country's GDP, even if that output actually belongs to people in another country. For example, all of the output of US multinationals in Ireland is included in Irish GDP even though a very high proportion of that output (the profit element) belongs to American parent companies. Irish GDP exceeds Irish GNP by circa 25 per cent.

GNP – Gross national product, a measure of a country's annual economic output using an ownership concept of output. So the profit element of the output of Irish-based US multinationals is included in US GNP and excluded from Irish GNP.

Government deficit – the gap between government spending and revenue when spending exceeds revenue.

IMF – International Monetary Fund.

Internal devaluation/revaluation – internal devaluation is where deflationary pressures in an economy cannot be accommodated by a fall in its external exchange rate. For domestic prices and wages to fall in international (i.e. external) terms they must also therefore fall in domestic (i.e. internal) terms. This can be economically dangerous as prices and incomes may fall sharply relative to domestic debts, causing a cascade of bankruptcies. Internal revaluation is where inflationary pressures in an economy are accommodated by a rise in its internal prices and wage levels. Internal devaluation and revaluation stand in contrast to external devaluation/revaluation (see above).

Keynesianism – this is the school of economic thought started by John Maynard Keynes. He advocated increased government expenditure and lowered taxes to stimulate demand and pull the economy out of the Great Depression.

Liquidity – the question of whether a person or entity has enough access to cash. Often a liquidity problem can be a symptom of a solvency problem.

Monetarism – this is the school of economic thought associated with Milton Friedman. He argued that the government should keep the money supply fairly steady, expanding it slightly each year, mainly to allow for the natural growth of the economy. If you allow money supply to grow too fast, inflation threatens; grow it too slow and recession or even depression can threaten.

NAMA – National Asset Management Agency. This is the government body set up to acquire and manage the property loans of the main Irish banks. By 2009 that category of loans had become hopelessly distressed. It was hoped that, by taking these mainly distressed loans off their hands, the banks would then be able to focus on their main job, i.e. lending to Irish companies, households and individuals.

Net wealth – this is derived by subtracting a person's total liabilities from their total assets. If a person's total liabilities exceed the value of their total assets they are said to have negative equity.

Nominal GDP – this is GDP (see above) measured at current prices, i.e. including the effects of inflation. Real GDP measures GDP after stripping out the effects of inflation. For example, if nominal GDP grew by 5 per cent but inflation over the same period was 3 per cent, real GDP would only have grown by 2 per cent.

Primary deficit or surplus – the balance of a government's spending and revenue before consideration of its interest bill. This is considered important because once a country reaches a primary surplus – as Ireland is expected to in 2014 – it is, in effect, only entering into fresh borrowings in order to finance the interest burden of past borrowings. It is no longer borrowing to finance day-to-day spending. This is the point at which borrowers can be less easily cowed by lenders threatening to withdraw credit.

Promissory notes – a form of IOU used instead of cash. For instance, when the Irish government invested additional monies in Anglo-Irish Bank in 2009 and 2010 it didn't use cash to do so. Instead it gave Anglo-Irish Bank a promissory note.

Real interest rates – this measures interest rates after deducting inflation.

REER – real effective exchange rate. This measures a country's exchange rate adjusted for inflation. If it rises, a country is becoming more expensive relative to the rest of the world. If it falls, a country is becoming more cost competitive relative to the rest of the world.

Rent yield – rent yields take the rental income that could be earned from a property and divide it by the property's price or value. So, for example, annual rental income of €15,000 earned from a property with a value of €200,000 would represent a rent yield of 7.5 per cent.

Solvency – the question of whether a person or entity has enough equity or net assets, i.e. whether the value of assets sufficiently exceeds the value of liabilities.

Taylor Rule – this is an economic rule of thumb that is used to estimate the appropriate central bank policy rate for an economy. It uses two variables: a country's inflation rate and the amount of spare economic capacity. The higher the inflation rate, the higher a country's interest rate should be. And the more spare economic capacity a country has, the lower its interest rate should be.

NOTES

Introduction (PAGES 1–5)

1. Irish Fiscal Advisory Council (2013), Fiscal Assessment Report, November, available from: www.fiscalcouncil.ie/fiscal-assessment-report- november-2/, accessed January 2014.
2. Claire Jones (2014), 'Too early to declare crisis over, says Draghi', *Financial Times*, 14 January, available from: http://www.ft.com/intl/cms/s/0/87f1e124-7909-11e3-b381-00144feabdc0.html#axzz2rLQN3xhM, accessed January 2014.
3. Kevin O'Rourke (2014), 'The euro zone needs a history lesson', *The Economist*, 17 January, available from: http://www.economist.com/blogs/freeexchange/2014/01/deflation-euro-zone-2, accessed January 2014.
4. Ambrose Evans-Pritchard (2014), 'Crippled eurozone to face fresh debt crisis this year, warns ex-ECB Strongman Axel Weber', *Daily Telegraph*, available from: http://www.telegraph.co.uk/finance/financetopics/davos/10590134/Crippled-eurozone-to-face-fresh-debt-crisis-this-year-warns-ex-ECB-strongman-Axel-Weber.html, accessed January 2014.
5. Szu Ping Chan (2014), 'France could destroy the euro, says Christopher Pissarides', *Daily Telegraph*, 25 January, available from: http://www.telegraph.co.uk/finance/financialcrisis/10596755/France-could-destroy-the-euro-says-Christopher-Pissarides.html, accessed January 2014.
6. Author's translation of interview with David Böcking und Stefan Kaiser, 2014, 'US-Ökonom Eichengreen: "Europa könnte 2014 in die Luft fliegen"', *der Spiegel*, 25 January, available from: http://www.spiegel.de/wirtschaft/soziales/us-oekonom-eichengreen-warnt-vor-einer-rueckkehr-der-euro-krise-a-945045.html, accessed January 2014.

Chapter 1: Is the Worst Behind Us? (PAGES 6–18)

1. Statement by Minister for Finance Brian Lenihan, 8 July 2008, available from: http://www.finance.gov.ie/viewdoc.asp?DocID=5370, accessed January 2014.
2. Government statement, 30 September 2008, available from: http://www.financialregulator.ie/press-area/press-releases/Pages/GovernmentDecisiontoSafeguardIrishBankingSystem.aspx, accessed January 2014.

3. Financial Statement of the Minister for Finance, 9 December 2009, available from: http://www.budget.gov.ie/budgets/2010/financial statement.aspx, accessed January 2014.

4. Minister for Finance speech to Financial Services Ireland Annual Launch, 4 July 2013, available from: http://www.finance.gov.ie/viewdoc. asp?DocID=7731, accessed January 2014.

5. Mary Minihan (2013), 'Enda Kenny: "This will be the last difficult budget"', Irish Times, 19 July, available from: http://www.irishtimes. com/news/politics/enda-kenny-this-will-be-the-last-difficult-budget-1.1468914, accessed January 2014.

6. Department of Finance, December 2009, 'Stability Programme Update', available from: http://www.budget.gov.ie/Budgets/2010/Documents/Final%20SPU.pdf, accessed January 2014. Table 4, p. 10.

7. Department of Finance, 'Budget 2013 – Economic and Fiscal Outlook', available from: http://budget.gov.ie/Budgets/2013/Documents/Budget%202013%20-%20Economic%20and%20Fiscal%20Outlook.pdf, accessed January 2014. Table 1, p. C5.

8. CSO (2013), 'Quarterly National Accounts: Quarter 1, 2013', 27 June 2013, available from: http://www.cso.ie/en/media/csoie/releasespublications/documents/latestheadlinefigures/qna_q12013.pdf, accessed January 2014. Annual growth rate derived from quarterly GDP data shown in Table 3.

9. Minister for Finance speech to Financial Services Ireland Annual Launch, 4 July 2013, available from: http://www.finance.gov.ie/viewdoc. asp?DocID=7731, accessed January 2014.

10. Financial Statement of the Minister for Finance,7 December 2010,available from: http://www.budget.gov.ie/budgets/2011/FinancialStatement.aspx, accessed January 2014.

11. Minister for Finance speech to Financial Services Ireland Annual Launch, 4 July 2013, available from: http://www.finance.gov.ie/viewdoc. asp?DocID=7731, accessed January 2014.

12. RTÉ (2011), 'Ireland wins concessions on bailout rate', 16 September, available from: http://www.rte.ie/news/2011/0916/306216-economy/, accessed January 2014.

13. Thejournal.ie (2013), 'As it happened: Michael Noonan and Brendan Howlin on promissory note deal', 7 February, available from: http://www.thejournal.ie, accessed January 2014.

14. Irish Fiscal Advisory Council (2013), Fiscal Assessment Report, April, available from: http://www.fiscalcouncil.ie/publications/fiscal-assessment-report-April-2013, accessed January 2014, p. 71.

15. IMF (2013), Ireland: Tenth Review Under the Extended Arrangement, June, available from: http://www.imf.org/external/pubs/ft/scr/2013/cr13163.pdf, accessed January 2014, p. 43.

16. Department of Finance (2010), *EU/IMF Programme of Financial Support for Ireland*, December, available from: http://www.finance.gov.ie, accessed January 2014.

17. Author's calculations based on Central Bank data.

18. John Eager FCA (2011), 'Legacy Debts: An SME Perspective', *Accountancy Ireland*, December, available from: http://www.accountancyireland.ie/Archive/2011, accessed January 2014.

19. RTÉ (2013), 'Half of loans to SMEs are non-performing', 11 April, available from: http://www.rte.ie/news/business, accessed January 2014.

20. Central Bank (2013), Residential Mortgage Arrears and Residential Statistics: Q3 2013, available from: www.centralbank.ie/press-area/press-releases/pages/residentialmortgagearrearsandrepossessionsstatistics Q32013.aspx, accessed January 2014.

21. IMF (2013), *Ireland: Tenth Review Under the Extended Arrangement*, June, available from: http://www.imf.org/external/pubs/ft/scr/2013/cr13163.pdf, accessed January 2014, p. 42.

22. Ciarán Hancock (2013), 'Michael Noonan signals stress tests for banks next year', *Irish Times*, 14 June, available from: http://www.irishtimes.com/business, accessed January 2014.

23. http://www.eurotreaties.com/maastrichtext.html, accessed January 2014.

24. Dan White (2013), 'Taxpayer beware! Irish banks need another €30bn at least', *Irish Independent*, 5 May, available from: http://www.independent.ie/business, accessed January 2014.

25. CSO (2013), *Quarterly National Household Survey*, November, available from: www.cso.ie, accessed January 2014.

26. Between 2008 and 2012, 358,100 people emigrated from Ireland at an annual rate of about 70,000. This compares with annual emigration of about 30,000 in the years 2002 to 2007. Increased annual emigration of about 40,000 over the five years 2008 to 2012 meant that there were around 200,000 fewer people living in Ireland by the end of 2012 than there would have been under previous emigration patterns.

27. Richard Colwell (2013), 'Gains for government parties suggest potential for future growth', 25 November, available from: http://www.redcresearch.ie, accessed January 2014.

28. IMF (2013), 'Euro Area Policies', Selected Issues Paper, July, available from: http://www.imf.org, accessed January 2014.

Chapter 2: Boom (PAGES 19–48)

1. http://www.anpost.ie/AnPost/History+and+Heritage, accessed January 2014.

2. 'Membership of EEC: Motion', Dáil Éireann Debate, vol. 259, no. 13, 21 March 1972, available from: http://oireachtasdebates.oireachtas.ie, accessed January 2014.

3. 'European Council Meeting: Statement by Taoiseach', Dáil Éireann Debate, vol. 312, no. 10, 15 March 1979, available from: http://oireachtasdebates.oireachtas.ie, accessed January 2014.

4. Fintan O'Toole (2013), 'Parliamentary accountability: a nefarious British Plot', 16 July, available from: http://www.irishtimes.com/news/politics, accessed January 2014.

5. Quoted in Christopher Booker and Richard North (2003), *The Great Deception – The Secret History of the European Union*, London: Continuum, p. 1.

6. http://ec.europa.eu/economy_finance/emu_history/documents/treaties/rometreaty2.pdf, accessed January 2014.

7. http://www.nobelprize.org/nobel_prizes/peace/laureates/2012/

8. 'Eleventh Amendment of the Constitution Bill, 1992: Second Stage', Dáil Éireann Debate, vol. 419, no. 1, 5 May 1992, available from: http://oireachtasdebates.oireachtas.ie, accessed January 2014.

9. 'Eleventh Amendment of the Constitution Bill, 1992: Second Stage – Resumed', Dáil Éireann Debate, vol. 419, no. 3, 7 May 1992, available from: http://oireachtasdebates.oireachtas.ie, accessed January 2014.

10. 'Eleventh Amendment of the Constitution Bill, 1992: Second Stage – Resumed'.

11. André Szász, quoted in David Marsh (2013), *Europe's Deadlock: How the Euro Crisis Could be Solved – and Why It Won't Happen*, New Haven, US: Yale University Press, p. 43.

12. Bill Jamieson (1994), *Britain Beyond Europe*, London: Duckworth, p. 72.

13. Jeffrey A. Frankel and Andrew K. Rose (1997), 'The Endogenity of the Optimum Currency Area Criteria', *The Economic Journal*, vol. 108, no. 449, pp. 1009–1025.

14. Quoted in David Marsh (2009), *The Euro – the Politics of the New Global Currency*, New Haven, US: Yale University Press, p. 200.

15. Quoted in Johan van Overtveldt (2011), *The End of the Euro – The Uneasy Future of the European Union*, Evanston, US: B2 Books, p. 52.

16. Quoted in van Overtveldt, *The End of the Euro*, p. 52.

17. http://www.spiegel.de/spiegel/print/d-9247341.html, author's translation.

18. JP Morgan (2012), 'Eye on the Market', 2 May, available from: http://www.sshermanassociates.com, accessed January 2014.

19. Rossa White (2005), 'Ireland's Interest Rate Should Be 6%', Davy Stockbrokers, 24 January, available from: www.davy.ie, accessed January 2014, p. 1.

20. White (2005), 'Ireland's Interest Rate Should Be 6%', Davy Stockbrokers, p. 2.
21. 'Eleventh Amendment of the Constitution Bill, 1992: Second Stage', Dáil Éireann Debate, vol. 419, no. 1, 5 May 1992, available from: http://oireachtasdebates.oireachtas.ie, accessed January 2014.
22. RTÉ (1999), 'Noonan advises government to pay attention to Central Bank Governor', 30 April, available from: http://www.rte.ie/news/1999/0430/1505-mortgage, accessed January 2014.
23. The export sales relief scheme taxed corporations at a rate of 0 per cent on profits made from export activities.
24. CSO data from various Statistical Yearbooks.
25. RTÉ (2011), 'Cabinet overruled Department of Finance warnings', 1 March, available from: http://www.rte.ie/news/2011/0301/298205-finance/, accessed January 2014.
26. The Independent Review Panel (2010), Strengthening the Capacity of the Department of Finance, December, http://www.finance.gov.ie/documents/publications/reports/2011/deptreview.pdf, accessed January 2014, p. 29.
27. Department of Finance (2005), 'Economic Review and Outlook', available from: http://www.finance.gov.ie/viewdoc.asp?DocID=3483, accessed January 2014.
28. IMF (2006), Ireland: Staff Report for the 2006 Article IV Consultation, August, available from: http://www.imf.org/external/pubs/ft/scr/2006/cr06293.pdf, accessed January 2014, p. 3.
29. IMF (2006), Ireland: Financial System Stability Assessment Update, August, available from: http://www.imf.org/external/pubs/ft/scr/2006/cr06292.pdf, accessed January 2014, p. 1.
30. OECD (2006), Economic Survey of Ireland, March, available from: http://www.oecd.org/ireland/economicsurveyofireland2006.htm, accessed January 2014, p. 8.
31. In fact, Bank of Ireland's share price on 14 November was €6.20. This represents a 48 per cent drop from its peak share price of €11.88.
32. Central Bank (2007), Financial Stability Report, available from: http://www.centralbank.ie/publications/pages/financialstabilityreport.aspx, accessed January 2014, p. 11.
33. EU Commission (2008), Macro Fiscal Assessment – Ireland, March, available from: http://ec.europa.eu/economy_finance/publications/publication12213_en.pdf, accessed January 2014, p. 5.
34. Paul Volcker (2013), 'The Fed and Big Banking at the Crossroads', The New York Review of Books, 15 August, available from: http://www.nybooks.com, accessed January 2014.
35. Tom Lyons (2013), 'Irish Nationwide was the breeding ground for the abuse of power', Irish Independent, 11 August, available from: http://www.independent.ie, accessed January 2014.

Chapter 3: Bust (PAGES 49–79)

1. Rossa White (2006), 'Dublin house prices headed for 100 times rent earned', Davy Stockbrokers, 29 March, available from: www.davy.ie, accessed January 2014, p. 1.
2. White (2006), 'Dublin house prices headed for 100 times rent earned', p. 3.
3. Morgan Kelly (2007), 'Banking on very shaky foundations', *Irish Times*, 7 September.
4. A property's rent yield is its annual rent income divided by its capital value. For example, a property generating an annual rent of €30,000 that had a value of €1,000,000 would have a 3 per cent rent yield.
5. Richard Koo (2012), 'The World in Balance Sheet Recession', available from: http://ineteconomics.org, accessed January 2014, p. 19.
6. Koo (2012), 'The World in Balance Sheet Recession', p. 21.
7. Irving Fisher (1933), 'The Debt-Deflation Theory of Great Depressions', *Econometrica*, vol. 1, no. 4, p. 342.
8. Koo (2012), 'The World in Balance Sheet Recession', p. 36.
9. Koo (2012), 'The World in Balance Sheet Recession', p. 36.
10. *The Economist* (2009), 'Out of Keynes's shadow', 12 February.
11. Author's calculation of the two-year average of mortgage interest rate less inflation, based on CSO data.
12. Department of Environment, Community and Local Government data.
13. Department of Environment, Community and Local Government data.
14. Finfacts (2012), 'Irish house price fall from 2007 peak may be as high as 60%', 13 March, available from: http://www.finfacts.ie, accessed January 2014.
15. http://namawinelake.wordpress.com/2013/04/24/index-confirms-Irish-commercial-property-prices-continue-to-decline-jll-index-q12013, accessed January 2014.
16. Central Bank (2013), *Quarterly Financial Accounts*, Q 1, available from: http://www.centralbank.ie, accessed January 2014.
17. The Committee on Public Accounts published a set of official documents leading up to the bank guarantee. See http://www.oireachtas.ie.
18. PWC stated, 'Under the PWC highest stress scenario, Anglo's core equity and tier 1 ratios are projected to exceed regulatory minima (Tier 1 – 4%) at 30 September 2010 after taking account of operating profits and stressed impairments.' PWC (2009), *Project Atlas: Anglo-Irish Bank Corporation plc – Summary Report Extracts*, 20 February, available from: http://www.finance.gov.ie, accessed January 2014, p. 37.
19. Merrill Lynch email to Department of Finance, 29 September 2008, available from: http://www.oireachtas.ie/viewdoc.asp?fn=/documents/Committees30thDail/PAC/Reports/DocumentsReGuarantee/document3.pdf, accessed January 2014.

20. Patrick Honohan (2010), *The Irish Banking Crisis Regulatory and Financial Stability Policy* 2003–2008, 31 May, available from: http://www.bankinginquiry.gov.ie, accessed January 2014, p. 14.
21. Patrick Honohan (2009), 'What Went Wrong in Ireland?' Trinity College Dublin, May, available from: http://www.tcd.ie, accessed January 2014, p. 1.
22. Patrick Honohan (2010), *The Irish Banking Crisis Regulatory and Financial Stability Policy* 2003–2008, 31 May, available from: http://www.bankinginquiry.gov.ie, accessed January 2014, p. 32.
23. Klaus Regling and Max Watson (2010), *A Preliminary Report on The Sources of Ireland's Banking Crisis*, available from http://www.bankinginquiry.gov.ie/Preliminary%20Report%20into%20Ireland's%20Banking%20Crisis%2031%20May%202010.pdf, accessed January 2014, p. 5.
24. Regling and Watson (2010), *A Preliminary Report on The Sources of Ireland's Banking Crisis*, p. 5.
25. EU Commission (2008), *Macro Fiscal Assessment – Ireland*, March, available from http://ec.europa.eu/economy_finance/publications/publication12213_en.pdf accessed January 2014, p. 5.
26. Regling and Watson (2010), *A Preliminary Report on The Sources of Ireland's Banking Crisis*, p. 6.
27. Regling and Watson (2010), *A Preliminary Report on The Sources of Ireland's Banking Crisis*, p. 24.
28. The Independent Review Panel (2010), *Strengthening the Capacity of the Department of Finance*, December, http://www.finance.gov.ie, accessed January 2014, p. 4.
29. The Independent Review Panel (2010), *Strengthening the Capacity of the Department of Finance*, p. 5.
30. The Independent Review Panel (2010), *Strengthening the Capacity of the Department of Finance*, p. 5.
31. RTÉ (2011), 'Cabinet overruled Department of Finance warnings', March, available from: http://www.rte.ie/news/2011/0301/298205-finance/, accessed January 2014.
32. The Independent Review Panel (2010), *Strengthening the Capacity of the Department of Finance*, p. 5.
33. Commission of Investigation into the Banking Sector in Ireland (2011), *Mis-judging Risk: Cuases of the Systemic Banking Crisis in Ireland*, March, available from: http://www.bankinginquiry.gov.ie/Documents/Misjuding%20Risk%20-%20Causes%20of%20the%20Systemic%20Banking%20Crisis%20in%20Ireland.pdf, accessed January 2014, p. 1.
34. Commission of Investigation into the Banking Sector in Ireland (2011), *Mis-judging Risk*, p. i.

35. Commission of Investigation into the Banking Sector in Ireland (2011), *Mis-judging Risk*, p. vii.
36. Quoted in David Marsh (2009), *The Euro – The Politics of the New Global Currency*, New Haven, US: Yale University Press, p. 64.
37. Quoted in Marsh (2009), *The Euro – The Politics of the New Global Currency*, p. 252.

Chapter 4: Plan A (PAGES 80–120)

1. Patrick Honohan (2008), 'Another Lap for the Irish Hare?' June, available from: http://www.tcd.ie/Economics/staff/phonohan/Brussels%2008%20Thu.ppt, accessed January 2014, p. 2.
2. Patrick Honohan and Daniela Klingebiel (2000), 'Controlling the Fiscal Costs of Banking Crises', May, available from: http://www1.worldbank.org/finance/assets/images/depins02.pdf, accessed January 2014, p. 3.
3. Patrick Honohan (2010), 'The Irish Banking Crisis Regulatory and Financial Stability Policy 2003–2008', 31 May, available from: http://www.bankinginquiry.gov.ie, accessed January 2014, p. 32.
4. This pattern was mercilessly documented in Laura Slattery (2010), 'Banking crisis – how the costs have evolved', *Irish Times*, 1 October. This section draws heavily on Slattery's article.
5. Slattery (2010), 'Banking crisis – how the costs have evolved'.
6. Bank of Ireland, AIB, Irish Life & Permanent, Anglo Irish Bank, Irish Nationwide Building Society and EBS.
7. Department of Finance (2010), *EU/IMF Programme of Financial Support for Ireland*, December, available at: http://www.finance.gov.ie, accessed January 2014, pp. 2–4.
8. Central Bank (2011), *The Financial Measures Programme Report*, Table 6, p. 13.
9. Irish Central Bank data.
10. John Eager FCA (2011), 'Legacy Debts: An SME Perspective', *Accountancy Ireland*, December, available from: http://www.accountancyireland.ie, accessed January 2014.
11. Pat Leahy (2013), *The Price of Power – Inside Ireland's Crisis Coalition*, Dublin, Penguin Ireland, p. 131.
12. Fiscal Advisory Council (2013), Fiscal Assessment Report, April, available from: http://www.fiscalcouncil.ie/wp-content/uploads/2013/04/FARApr13.pdf, accessed January 2014, p. 49.
13. Reuters (2013), 'UPDATE 1: Merkel reins in plan to transfer powers to Brussels', June, available from: http://www.reuters.com/article/2013/06/02/germany-merkel-eu-idUSL5N0EE0QV20130602, accessed January 2014.
14. Joe Wiesenthal (2010), 'Merkel: There Is "No Possibility" Of Bailing Out Greece, Business Insider', February, available from: http://www.

businessinsider.com/angela-merkel-denies-greek-bailout-2010-2, accessed January 2014.

15. Quentin Peel, Richard Milne and Ralph Atkins (2011), 'Merkel bids to quash Greece default talk', *Financial Times*, September, available from: http://www.ft.com, accessed January 2014.

16. Jan Strupczewski (2013), 'Decision on third Greek bailout set for November: officials', September, available from: http://www.reuters. com/article/2013/09/05/us-eurozone-greece-idUSBRE9840NN20130905, accessed January 2014.

17. Bundesverfassungsgericht (2009), BvE 2/08 vom 30.6.2009, Absatz-Nr. (1 - 421), June, available from: http://www.bverfg.de/entscheidungen/ es20090630_2bve000208en.html, accessed January 2014.

18. Speech by Jean-Claude Trichet, President of the ECB, on receiving the Karlspreis 2011 in Aachen, 2 June 2011, available from: http://www.ecb. europa.eu/press/key/date/2011/html/sp110602.en.html, accessed January 2014.

19. RTÉ News (2013), '12.3% of mortgages in arrears – Central Bank', June, available from: http://www.rte.ie/news/business/2013/0621/457978-mortgage-arrears-march/, accessed January 2014.

20. Finance Minister Brian Lenihan (2009), Statement on the Economy to Dáil Éireann, 29 January, cached version available: http://finance.gov.ie, accessed January 2014.

21. Central Bank of Ireland (2013), 'Money and Banking Statistics: August 2013', September, available from: http://www.centralbank.ie/polstats/ stats/cmab/Documents/2013m08_ie_monthly_statistics.pdf, accessed January 2014.

22. Central Statistics Office (2013), *Residential Property Price Index – June 2013*, July, available from: http://www.cso.ie/en/media/csoie/ releasespublications/documents/prices/2013/rppi_jun2013.pdf, accessed January 2014, p. 1.

23. Goodbody Stockbrokers (2012), 'Irish Housing Market: What price is residential property really transacting for?' March, available from: http://www.allsop.co.uk/js/tiny_mce/plugins/filemanager/files/Irish_ Housing_Market_-_Goodbody.pdf, accessed January 2014, p. 1.

24. Finfacts (2012), 'Irish Economy 2012: Number of mortgage loans issued in second quarter at same level as in 1970', August, available from: http://www.finfacts.ie/irishfinancenews/article_1024783.shtml, accessed January 2014.

25. Jerome Reilly (2013), 'Huge Dublin property surge sparks frenetic bids', *Irish Independent*, 25 August, available from: http://www.independent. ie/business/irish/huge-dublin-property-surge-sparks-frenetic-bids-29525685.html, accessed January 2014.

26. Proinsias O'Mahony (2012), 'Facing facts about house repossessions', *Southern Star*, 31 March, available from: http://www.southernstar.ie/News/Facing-facts-about-house-repossessions-3343.htm, accessed January 2014.

27. Reuters (2013), 'Irish lenders moving too slow on arrears – Central Bank', 25 September, available from: http://www.reuters.com/article/2013/09/25/ireland-arrears-idUSWLA007T520130925, accessed January 2014.

28. Ciarán Hancock (2013), 'Price of Dublin houses to rise by 10%, predicts ESRI', *Irish Times*, 23 August, available from: http://www.irishtimes.com/business/sectors/financial-services/price-of-dublin-houses-to-rise-by-10-predicts-esri-1.1502779, accessed January 2014.

29. *Irish Examiner* (2005), 'Irish house prices are overvalued', 22 November, available from: http://www.irishexaminer.com/archives/2005/1122/ireland/ irish-house-prices-are-aposovervaluedapos-558764306.html, accessed January 2014.

30. Ulster Bank (2013), Northern Ireland Residential Property Price Index Q2 2013, August, available from: http://www.ulsterbankcapitalmarkets.com/Handlers/docstream.ashx?doc_id=2283, accessed January 2014.

31. 2007: NI price index 100% x €1.48 = €1.48. 2013: NI price index 34% (representing 66% drop) x €1.20 = €40.80.

32. Author's calculations based on ECB data available from: http://sdw.ecb.europa.eu/browse.do?node=2120781, accessed January 2014.

33. Net wealth or equity can simply be defined as the value of total assets less the value of total liabilities.

34. Mary Cussen and Gillian Phelan (2011), 'The Rise and Fall of Sectoral Net Wealth in Ireland', Central Bank Quarterly Bulletin Q2 2011, available from: http://www.financialregulator.ie/publications/Documents/The%20Rise%20and%20Fall%20of%20Sectoral%20Net%20Wealth%20in%20Ireland.pdf, accessed January 2014, p. 73.

35. Ireland's GNP in 2012 was €133 billion.

36. John Walsh (2013), 'Tracker mortgages costing banks €708m every year, research reveals', *Irish Examiner*, 20 July, available from: http://www.irishexaminer.com/business/tracker-mortgages-costing-banks-708m-every-year-research-reveals-237414.html, accessed January 2014.

37. *Irish Examiner* (2013), 'ECB wants to phase out loss making trackers', 26 September, available from: http://www.irishexaminer.com/business/ecb-wants-to-phase-out-loss-making-trackers-244317.html, accessed January 2014.

38. *Irish Times* (2013), 'Michael Noonan signals stress tests for Irish banks next year', 14 June, available from: http://www.irishtimes.com, accessed January 2014.

39. *Irish Examiner* (2012), 'Gilmore: Budget will put end of austerity in sight', 4 December, available from: http://www.irishexaminer.com/budget/

breaking/gilmore-budget-will-put-end-of-austerity-in-sight-576588.
html, accessed January 2014.

40. John Moran (2013), 'Alternatives to Austerity', speech given to MacGill
Summer School, 2 August, available from: http://www.finance.gov.ie,
accessed January 2014.

41. Dáilwatch.ie (2013), 'Budget 2014 must signal end of austerity in sight
– IBEC', 7 October, available from: http://www.dailwatch.ie/en-gb/
blog/2013-10-07/budget-2014-must-signal-end-austerity-sight-ibec-4,
accessed January 2014.

42. JP Morgan (2013), 'The Euroarea Adjustment: About Halfway There', 28
May.

43. Irish Fiscal Advisory Council (April 2013), *Fiscal Assessment Report*,
available from: http://www.fiscalcouncil.ie/publications/fiscal-assessment-
report-april-2013/, accessed January 2014, pp. 70–71.

44. International Monetary Fund (2013), *Ireland: Tenth Review Under
the Extended Arrangement*, June, available from: http://www.imf.org/
external/pubs/cat/longres.aspx?sk=40686.0, accessed January 2014, p. 1.

45. Irish Fiscal Advisory Council (April 2013), *Fiscal Assessment Report*, pp.
70–71.

46. National Treasury Management Agency (2012), *Annual Report and
Accounts for* 2012, available from: http://www.ntma.ie/publications/,
accessed January 2014.

47. Kevin H. O'Rourke and Alan M. Taylor (2013), 'Cross of Euros', *Journal
of Economic Perspectives*, vol. 27, no. 3, available from: http://pubs.
aeaweb.org/doi/pdfplus/10.1257/jep.27.3.167, accessed January 2014,
p. 180.

48. Rossa White (2005), 'Ireland's interest rate should be 6%', Davy
Stockbrokers Weekly Market Comment, 24 January, available from:
http://www.davy.ie/content/pubarticles/wmccr20050124.pdf, accessed
January 2014.

49. Caroline Baum (2012), 'Bernanke May Owe Milton and Anna Another
Apology', Bloomberg Opinion, 3 October, available from: http://www.
bloomberg.com/news/2012-10-03/bernanke-may-owe-milton-and-
anna-another-apology.html, accessed January 2014.

50. Milton Friedman (2006), 'Why Money Matters', *Hoover Digest*, 30
October, available from: http://www.hoover.org/publications/hoover-
digest/article/5993, accessed January 2014.

51. On 26 December 2008, for example, the euro reached £0.98 sterling.
With IR£1 equivalent to €1.27, this meant that IR£1 was worth £1.24
sterling on that day.

52. Fabrizio Saccomanni, quoted in Marsh (2013), *Europe's Deadlock, How
the Euro Crisis Could Be Solved – and Why It Won't Happen*, p. 89.

53. John Maynard Keynes (1925), 'The Economic Consequences of Mr Churchill', Royal Economic Society, pp. 10–13.

54. John Maynard Keynes (1920), *The Economic Consequences of the Peace*, New York: Howard Brace, p. 225.

55. J.J. Lee (1989), *Ireland 1912–1985: Politics and Society*, Cambridge: Cambridge University Press, p. 577.

56. Paul McCulley and Zoltan Pozsar (2012), 'Does Central Bank Independence Frustrate the Optimal Fiscal-Monetary Policy Mix in a Liquidity Trap?', available from: http://www.interdependence.org/wp-content/uploads/2012/03/Paul-McCulley-Fellows-Paper.pdf, accessed January 2014, p. 2.

57. Dermot T. O'Keary (2011), 'Deleveraging, banks and economic recovery', Goodbody Stockbrokers, October, available from: http://www.finfacts.ie/biz10/deleveraging_Irish_%20banks_economic_recovery.pdf, accessed January 2014, p. 30.

58. *The Economist* (2006), 'Milton Friedman, a giant among economists', 23 November, available from: http://www.economist.com, accessed January 2014.

59. Milton Friedman (1969), *Optimum Quantity of Money*, Chicago: Aldine Publishing Company, p. 4.

60. Quoted in Dermot Keogh (2008), *Jack Lynch*, Dublin, Gill & Macmillan, p. 100.

Chapter 5: Plan B (PAGES 121–59)

1. Andrew Kenningham (2011), 'Why do countries default and what are the consequences?' *Global Economic Focus*, London: Capital Economics, 7 July, chart 1, p. 2.

2. Sam Jones and Jude Webber (2012), 'Argentine navy ship seized in asset fight', *Financial Times*, 3 October, available from: http://www.ft.com, accessed January 2014.

3. Kenningham (2011), 'Why do countries default and what are the consequences?' p. 10.

4. David Marsh (2013), 'Germany would like the world to stop', 28 October, available from: http://www.marketwatch.com/story/germany-would-like-the-world-to-stop-2013-10-28, accessed January 2014.

5. Kenningham (2011), 'Why do countries default and what are the consequences?' table 2, p. 4.

6. Bianca De Paoli, Glenn Hoggarth and Victoria Saporta (2006), 'Costs of Sovereign Default', Bank of England, July.

7. Eduardo Borensztein and Ugo Panizza (2008), 'The Costs of Sovereign Default', IMF Working Paper, October.

8. Udaibir Das, Michael Papaioannou and Christopher Trebesch (2010), 'Sovereign Default Risk and Private Sector Access to Capital in Emerging Markets', IMF Working Paper, January.

9. Quoted in Marsh (2009), *The Euro – The Politics of the New Global Currency*, p. 150.

10. Roger Bootle (2012), 'Leaving the Euro: A Practical Guide', London: Capital Economics.

11. *The Economist* (2010), 'Default Settings', 31 March, available from: http://www.economist.com, accessed January 2014.

12. *The Economist* (2011), *'To default, or not to default?'* 20 June, available from: http://www.economist.com/blogs, accessed January 2014.

13. Kenningham (2011), 'Why do countries default and what are the consequences?' p. 17.

14. Michael B. Devereux (2003), 'A Tale of Two Currencies: The Asian Crisis and the Exchange Rate Regimes of Hong Kong and Singapore', *Review of International Economics*, vol. 11, no.1, pp. 38–54.

15. Mark Weisbrot, Rebecca Ray, Juan A. Montecino and Sara Kozameh (2011), 'The Argentine Success Story and its Implications', Center for Economic and Policy Research, October, available from www.cepr.net, accessed January 2014, p. 1.

16. Weisbrot, Ray, Montecino and Kozameh (2011), 'The Argentine Success Story and its Implications', p. 1.

17. Werner Baer, Diego Margot and Gabriel Montes-Rojas (2009), 'Argentina's Default and the Lack of Dire Consequences', City University London Department of Economics, Discussion Paper Series No. 10/09, available from http://www.city.ac.uk, p. 1.

18. Andrew K. Rose (2006), 'Checking Out: Exits from Currency Unions', December, available from: http://faculty.haas.berkeley.edu/arose/Exit.pdf, accessed January 2014, p. 1.

19. Daniel Hannan (2012), *A Doomed Marriage: Britain and Europe*, London: Notting Hill Editions, pp. 52–3.

20. Peter Garber and Michael Spencer (1994), 'The Dissolution of the Austro-Hungarian Empire: Lessons for Currency Reform', IMF Working Paper, available from: www.princeton.edu, accessed January 2014, pp. 33–4.

21. David Woo and Athanasios Vamvakidis (2012), 'Game theory and euro breakup risk premium', Bank of America Merrill Lynch, 10 July.

22. Woo and Vamvakidis (2012), 'Game theory and euro breakup risk premium', p. 8.

23. Norton Rose (2012), 'Redenomination Risk', August, available from: http://www.nortonrosefulbright.com/knowledge/publications/69597/redenomination-risk, accessed January 2014.

24. Pat Leahy (2013), *The Price of Power – Inside Ireland's Crisis Coalition*, pp. 131–2.

25. David Murphy (2013), 'What the Cypriot chaos means for Ireland', 9 April, available from: http://www.rte.ie/blogs/business/2013/03/19/what-the-cypriot-chaos-means-for-ireland/, accessed January 2014.

26. William L. Silber (2009), 'Why Did FDR's Bank Holiday Succeed?' available from: http://www.newyorkfed.org/research/epr/09v15n1/0907silb.pdf, accessed January 2014, p. 1.

27. Trading Economics (2014), 'Iceland Inflation Rate', available from: http://www.tradingeconomics.com/iceland/inflation-cpi, accessed January 2014.

28. http://www.clubdeparis.org, accessed January 2014.

29. http://www.clubdeparis.org, accessed January 2014.

30. http://www.eurocrisismonitor.com, accessed January 2014.

31. Central Bank (2013), statisitics available from: www.centralbank.ie/polstats/stats/cmab/documents/ie_table_a.4_credit_institutions_-_aggregate_balance_sheet.xls, accessed January 2014.

32. European Council (2011), Euro area summit statement, 29 June, available from: http://www.european-council.europa.eu/home-page/highlights/euro-area-summit-statement?lang=en, accessed January 2014.

33. Viral V. Acharya and Sascha Steffen (2013), 'The "Greatest" Carry Trade Ever? Understanding Eurozone Bank Risks', available from: http://pages.stern.nyu.edu/~sternfin/vacharya/public_html/pdfs/201300421_Carry%20Trade%20Paper.pdf, accessed January 2014, p. 1.

34. *Irish Times* (2013), 'End of austerity budgets near – claims Noonan', 5 July, available from: http://www.irishtimes.com, accessed January 2014.

35. Quoted in Christopher Bookerand Richard North (2003), *The Great Deception – The Secret History of the European Union*, London: Continuum, p. 121.

36. Phoebus Athanassiou (2009), 'Withdrawal and Expulsion from the EU and EMU: Some Reflections', European Central Bank Legal Working Paper, series no. 10, December, available from: http://www.ecb.europa.eu/pub/pdf/scplps/ecblwp10.pdf, accessed January 2014, p. 18.

37. Athanassiou (2009), 'Withdrawal and Expulsion from the EU and EMU: Some Reflections', p. 19.

38. Damian McBride (2013), ' "I'll put troops on the streets": Gordon Brown's spin doctor reveals just how close to anarchy Britain came when the banks crashed', *Daily Mail*, 20 September, available from: http://www.dailymail.co.uk/news/article-2427617/Gordon-Brown-considered-putting-troops-streets-banks-crashed-reveals-Damian-McBride.html, accessed January 2014.

39. Speech made at the annual meeting of the IMF in Washington, September 2011.
40. http://www.eurocrisismonitor.com, accessed January 2014.
41. Variant Perception (2012), 'A Primer on the Euro Breakup: Depart, Default, and Devalue as the Optimal Solution', London, July, p. 56.
42. http://www.ifsc.ie/page.aspx?idpage=17, accessed January 2014.

Chapter 6: Epilogue (PAGES 160–67)
1. Wolfgang Herles (2005), *Wir sind kein Volk. Eine Polemik*, Munich: Piper Taschenbuch.
2. *Die Welt* (2004), 'Karl Otto Pöhl ist überzeugt: "Der Kurs beim Umtausch war verhängnisvoll"', Berlin, 29 August, available from: http://www.welt.de/print-wams/article115077/Karl-Otto-Poehl-ist-ueberzeugt-Der-Kurs-beim-Umtausch-war-verhaengnisvoll.html, accessed January 2014.
3. Quoted in Shane Fitzgerald (2011), 'A Euro Finance Ministry?' Blog of The Institute of International and European Affairs, Dublin, available from: http://www.iiea.com/blogosphere/a-euro-finance-ministry, accessed January 2014.
4. Fitzgerald (2011), 'A Euro Finance Ministry?'
5. Mark Paul (2013), 'Ex-Bush adviser predicts 20-year economic slump for Ireland', *Irish Times*, 2 October, available from: http://www.irishtimes.com/business/sectors/financial-services/ex-bush-adviser-predicts-20-year-economic-slump-for-ireland-1.1546629, accessed January 2014.
6. Quoted in David J. Lynch (2010), *When the Luck of the Irish Ran Out*, London: Palgrave Macmillan, p. 68.